MERKX+GIROD: INTERIOR ARCHITECTS

Birkhäuser – Publishers for Architecture
Basel·Boston·Berlin

Frame Publishers, Amsterdam

HIGHS

Two phases of a project stand out for the enjoyment they offer: the period in which you make the first sketches of the space, when everything still lies ahead of you, and the phase in which you select the materials. Choosing materials, colours, finishes – terrific! In between is more work than you care to imagine.

EVELYNE MERKX

When you get the feeling – even though the problem may still be extremely complicated – that you're headed in the right direction, the high is unbelievable. Of course, having the opportunity to realise a winning competition entry isn't bad either. A good example is the time we were notified, only a half-hour after presenting our project to the Council of State committee, that we'd won by an unanimous vote. Sensational – the thrill that comes with winning the gold medal – but completely different from the instant the fog lifts. As far as I'm concerned, that particular feeling is the real moment of triumph.

PATRICE GIROD

HOW IT ALL BEGAN

In the wake of my divorce – having finally, finally decided to apply for admission to the Rietveld Academy in Amsterdam, in the hope of studying interior architecture – I found myself filled with doubt. A woman with two kids is exactly what they're looking for, I thought ironically.

I already had what seemed like an entire life behind me. For years I was sales-promotion project manager for De Bijenkorf department store, after which I followed my husband abroad. Our children were born while we were still out of the country. After a period in America and one in Germany, I returned to the Netherlands, both children in tow, at the age of 32. *My* turn.

Entrance examination for the Rietveld Academy. Fortunately, we were given a special assignment: a self-portrait. I sawed a bunch of wood into blocks, reassembled the pieces and glued photos onto the surfaces. My favourite recipe on one side, a building I was crazy about on another, and so forth. A puzzle. During the interview, I turned the blocks this way and that, making sure that the photos were visible. Then I dumped the blocks in a sack, tied it with a knot and handed it over: my self-portrait. A short time later I received a letter of acceptance. At long last.

EVELYNE MERKX

I knew I wanted to be an architect when I was six years old. Thanks to an interest in building and technology, my father had collected a lot of books on the subject, and even as a small boy, I pored over the illustrations. I recall being especially impressed by the luxury liner *Le Normandie*. So modern. Such tremendous opulence.

Le Corbusier also made a big impact on me as a boy. At the beginning of the war my father, who was in the French army, was transferred from one base to another. The family moved with him, and one of the houses we stayed in was an example of *Neue Sachlichkeit*. I was positively over the moon.

Born into an international family in Strasbourg – his mother was Dutch, his father French – Patrice Girod moved to the Netherlands at the age of 11.

PATRICE GIROD

PROBLEMS GALORE

2 Each project is actually an accumulation of problems, each of which has to be solved. Evelyne and I are usually on the same wavelength during the early phase. Our disagreements, which emerge during the smaller steps that follow, are a necessary part of the process. Arguing things out makes the work better. No, it's not about getting one's own way; it's a matter of debate.

PATRICE GIROD

3

SUPERFLUOUS

Some people see us as posh designer dollies. An interesting observation, but irrelevant. Furthermore, it's an opinion that I ab-so-lute-ly dispute. Buildings will always have to be adapted to new users or to the demands of a different age, and doing that well is an art.

EVELYNE MERKX

ADDED VALUE

The added value that we give our clients is the knowledge that from the very beginning, the space and what it contains are a coherent entity. This leads to complex discussions with contractors, who aren't used to this type of unified approach, but the result provides a much higher level of consistency.

PATRICE GIROD

SIGNATURE

Our signature. That's a term we hear a lot. Unfortunately it's always about workmanship, while spatial interventions are often overlooked. Too bad, because that's our area of expertise.
When I design a restaurant, I start by moulding the space and shaping the skin. Only when I get *that* right do I add an exciting element. One example is Plancius, with its long display case for bottled water. Another is the wallpapered bays at De Bijenkorf in The Hague. Finishing touches.
There's nothing wrong with using trendy colours and materials. When they're due for refurbishment, you change them. Pick up a paintbrush. Nothing to it. But the space itself – take the HEMA department store on Nieuwendijk, for instance – will be around for at least 50 years.

EVELYNE MERKX

GETTING STARTED

'Good Lord! There's so much I don't know' – that was one of my initial discoveries after graduating. The academy helps you to develop an identity. After that you get the – very sobering – opportunity to practice your new profession.
You must learn how to calculate, how to instruct a contractor – as it happens, contractors often don't want what you want; they want the job done fast, and fast means unfortunately often sloppy – how to do everything. In the early stages, I was on top of it all. I wanted to know everything. Absolutely everything. It's different now. Experience has made me wiser, and I have people to help me. That's a calming thought, but it's not as great as it sounds. With several large assignments at the same time, you sometimes get the feeling you've lost grip on the situation. And that grip is exactly what appeals to me. So I still manage to find time to 'take a look at the tiling', something I like to do.

EVELYNE MERKX

You get under way, but you don't know a bloody thing. Making a simple floor plan – something still done by hand when I started out – isn't so difficult, but covering all the building specifications… Forget it.

PATRICE GIROD

AN EYE FOR THE INTERIOR

4 I have more respect for good interior architecture than I do for good architecture. An interior architect needs to have both an understanding of architecture and an eye for specific subtleties. Refinement, care, detail – three core values.

PATRICE GIROD

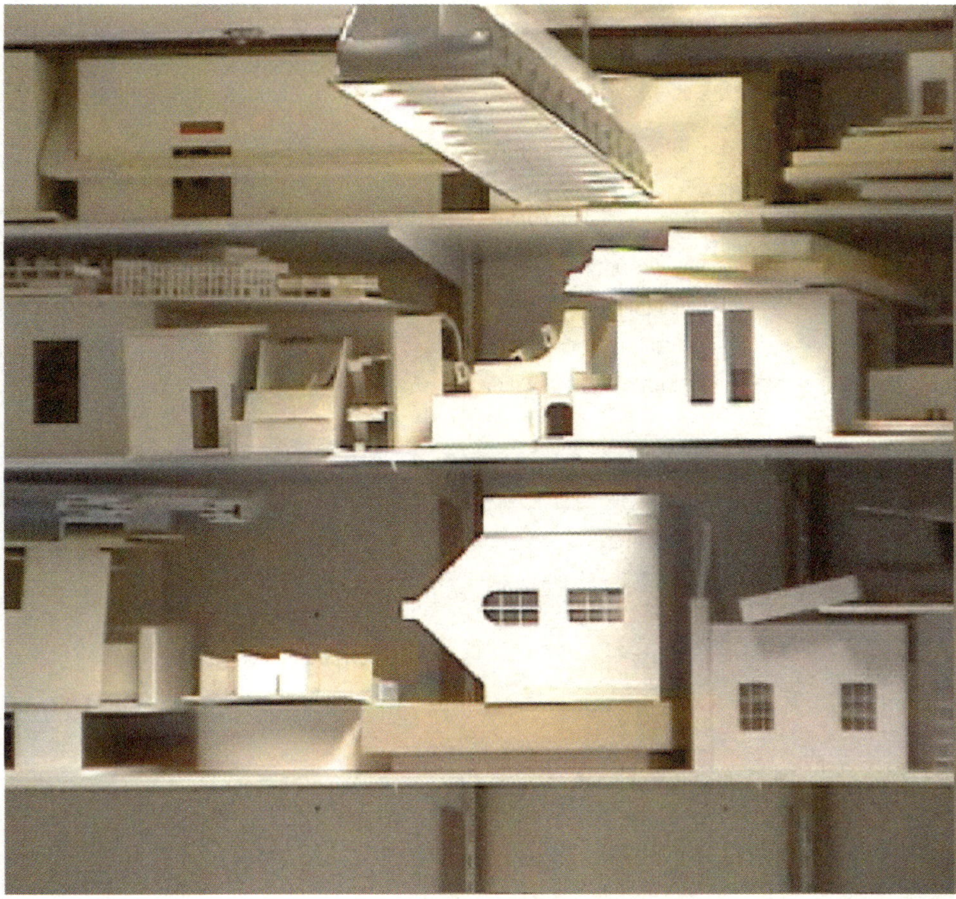
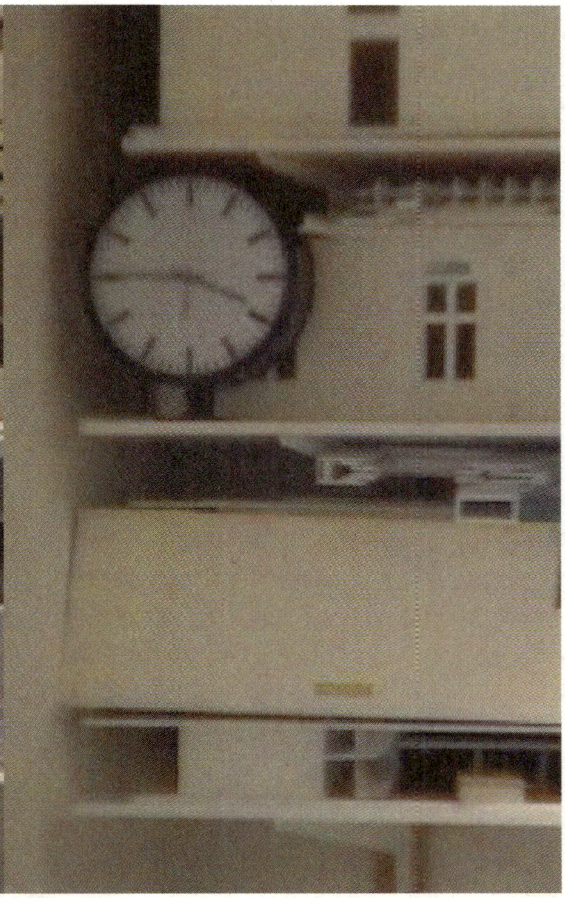
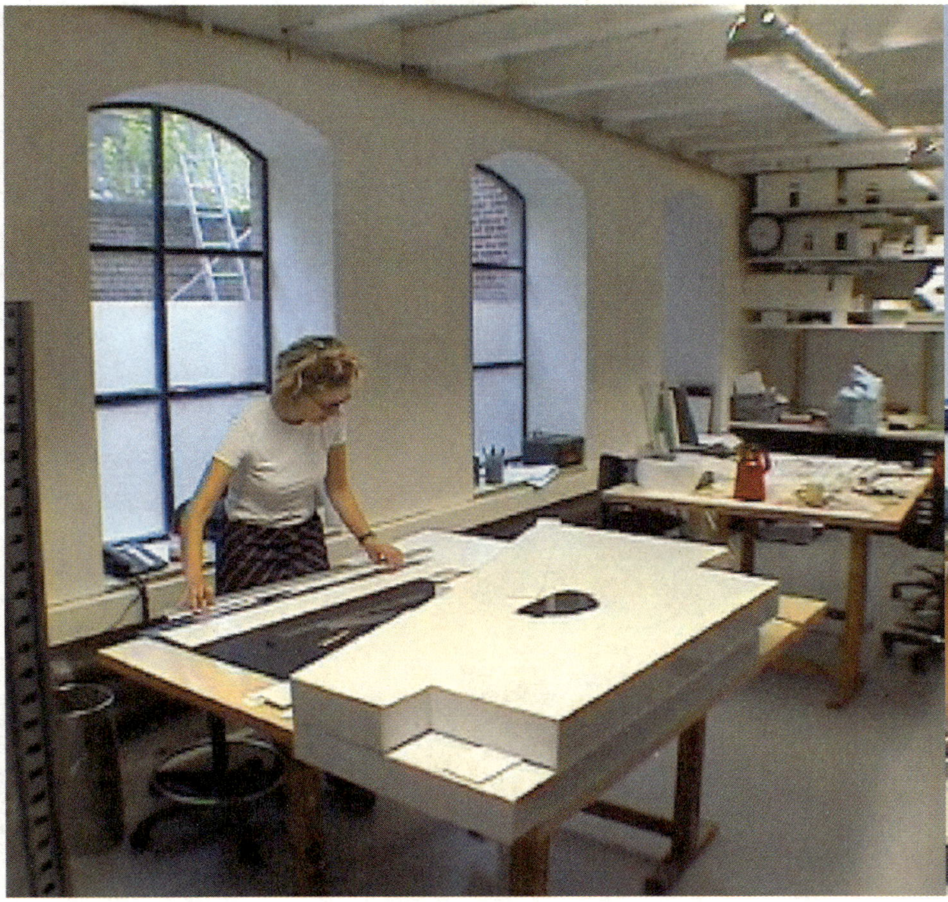
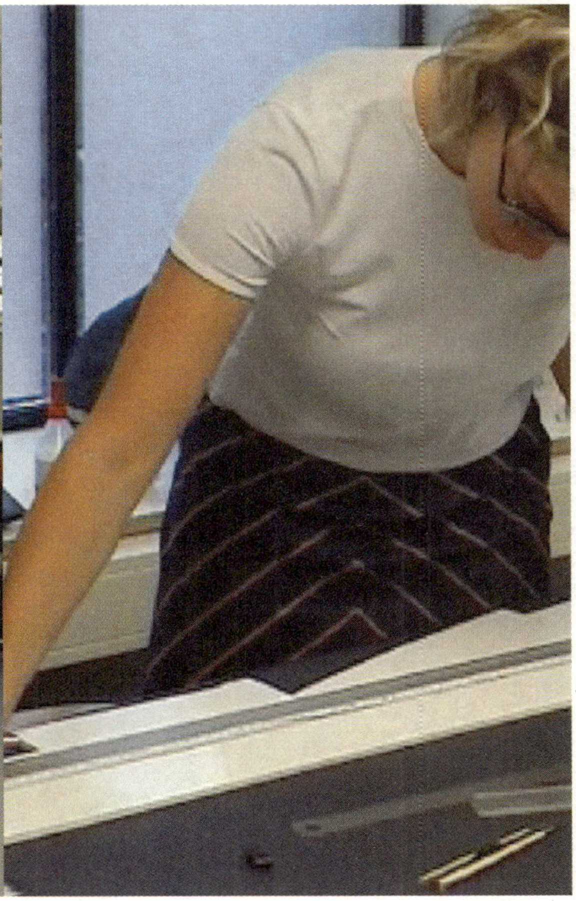

INVERSELY PROPORTIONAL
What it's all about? Giving a space an extra dimension.

EVELYNE MERKX

Ultimately, it has to do with a feeling for detail.

PATRICE GIROD

SYNERGY
In terms of both vocabulary and behaviour, we seem to be complementing each other more every day. I've been noticing it in our work for the Trêves Hall project. Evelyne has a fantastic eye for how things go together, for which elements are important, for those things that can be connected, opened up, extended. All spatial interventions.

PATRICE GIROD

THEY MEET
Contrary to what everyone seems to think, we didn't meet at the Rietveld Academy in Amsterdam. When Patrice applied for the position of instructor in architectonic design, as successor to Jan Rietveld, I had already graduated. Interestingly, at that time someone *did* ask me what I thought of him, but only because I had made a number of models for Girod-Groeneveld Architects.

EVELYNE MERKX

SOAP FACTORY
As soon as I graduated, I went into business for myself. I had to move out of the place where I'd been living, because it was too expensive and too small to function as both home and workplace. Combining the two was a must if I wanted to care for my children and still manage to work evenings. On top of all that, I was borderline broke. An artist friend told me about an attic space in a former soap factory in the centre of the Jordaan. It was an enormous shambles. Even the estate agent called it 'a pigsty'. But I took the leap, and it was the right thing to do. I'm still at the same address.
We have no private parking place, no chic reception area – just the choice of a tiny lift or four flights of stairs. This is a workplace, with the emphasis on *work*. And that goes for the other businesses in this enormous building as well. The place is filled with photographers, designers and the like. My workspace used to be right next to our living room, and there was no hiding the fact. The glass doors separating the two were open much of the time. Most clients had no problem with the situation. If they did, it was a sign that we were not really right for each other.

EVELYNE MERKX

HIS VIEW OF HER
Evelyne's treatment of colour, materials and styling is truly exceptional. I'm not in the same league at all. It's like music, which I love madly, even though I don't play an instrument. And for that very reason I think someone who's a good musician is terribly clever.
Not only does Evelyne have taste, vision and a sense of refinement; her mind is always several steps ahead of the game, and she rarely opts for the obvious.

PATRICE GIROD

WISHES
6 I'd absolutely love to do a movie theatre; and together we dream of doing a hotel design.

PATRICE GIROD

Yeah, a hotel. Cool. I hope they call us.

EVELYNE MERKX

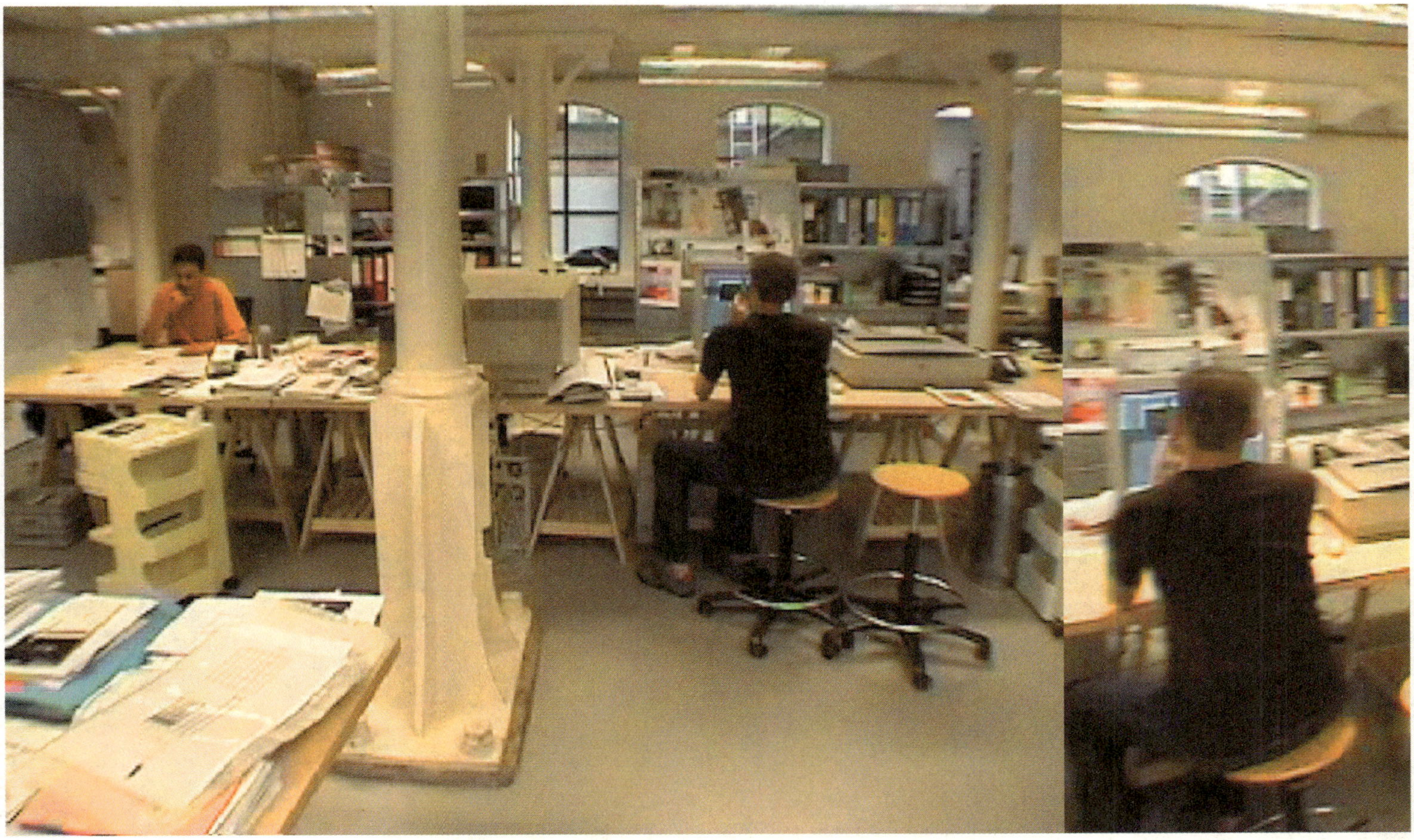

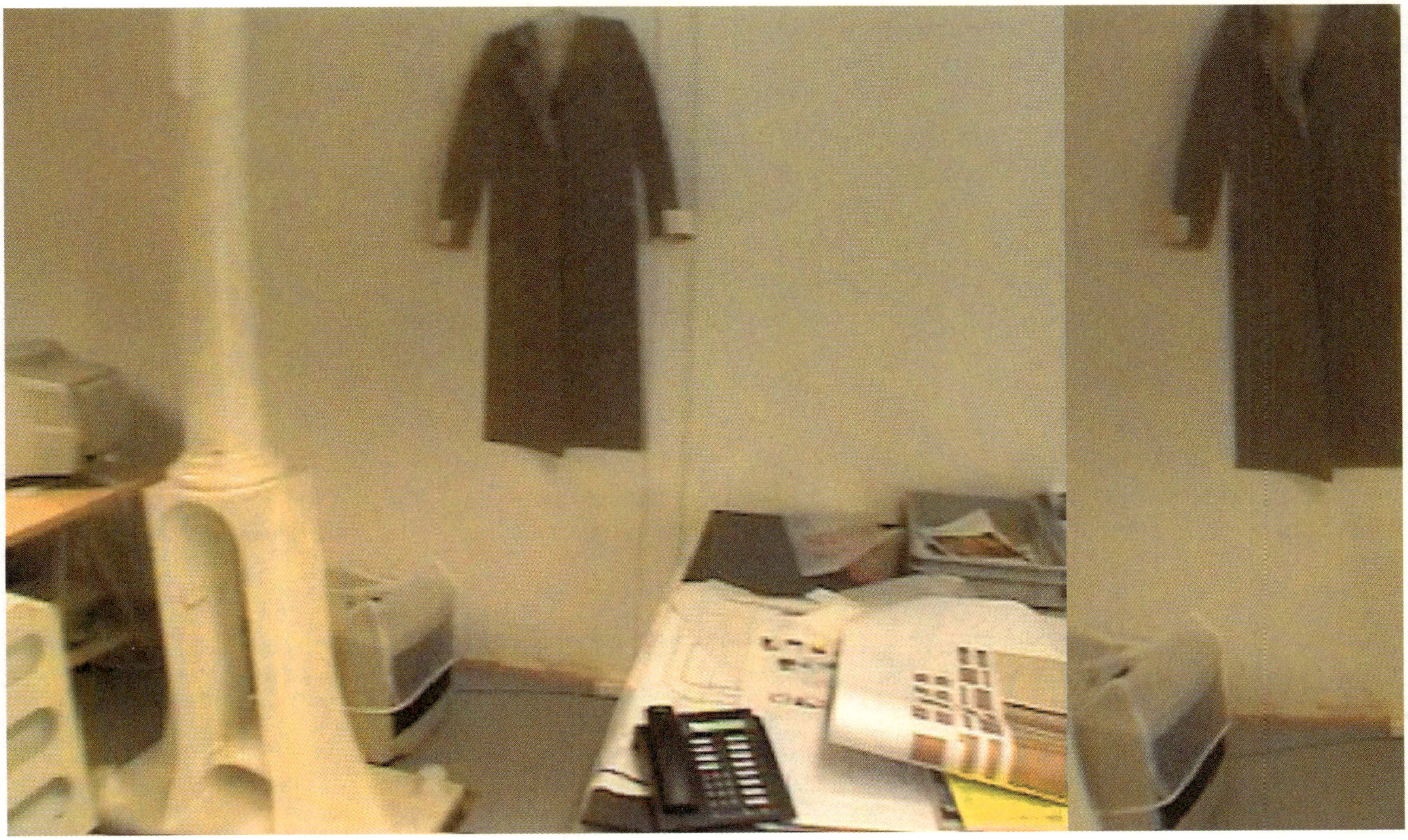

Building a house together is another dream of mine. But I don't really see it happening. We're far too attached to Amsterdam.

EVELYNE MERKX

THE PREFERRED CLIENT
A good client is a person with ambitions. Conviction, a desire that engenders a response – these are more important than money. It's not interesting to be given carte blanche. I'm not the kind of architect who sits around on Sunday afternoons designing something for fun. I need the field of tension that exists between architect and client.

PATRICE GIROD

MIX
Our greatest similarity? We're both convinced that you can add something new to something old. Long before I arrived on the scene, Patrice did just that in the canalside property that he and Abel Cahen built. New materials? A contemporary language of form? Anything goes as long as you pay attention to good proportions. How do you do it? Ask the designer.

EVELYNE MERKX

BAGGAGE AND MORE BAGGAGE
When I look at a new project, I look with everything I've got. In one hand I hold the existing situation, including its limitations; in the other lies all the possibilities in the world – every single opportunity.

EVELYNE MERKX

INTERACTION
We confer with each other a lot – track down an empty table, start talking and immediately put our ideas into sketches. New commissions often revolve around interior architecture, so sometimes I'm the one who takes an initial look at the situation. Often we go together. Back at the office, we have in-depth conversations about what we've seen. Frequently our 'brothers-in-arms' are involved as well.

EVELYNE MERKX

SHAKE UP
Employees need a good shaking up every so often. 'Get away from that computer, grab a pen, start from scratch this time. Show us something we've never seen before.'

EVELYNE MERKX

NO SIDE ISSUES
There are no side issues in this business, just main issues. Whether or not something works depends on the design as a whole. Every component is essential. Details are just as important as the big picture.

EVELYNE MERKX

EXTREMES
'Tempestuous' is a word often used to describe me – a term that's liable to scare new clients. Fortunately there's also Patrice, the imperturbable pragmatic. And the list of our projects, of course, which by now creates a sense of confidence in advance.

EVELYNE MERKX

DETAILS
8 Good hinges and locks, nice joinery, enamelled signs... I love details. People sometimes say that I should have been born in an earlier century.

EVELYNE MERKX

STYLE
A quintessential Merkx+Girod style? Perhaps, but I always consider the building in question. The Concertgebouw, for instance, demands ornament. And even though

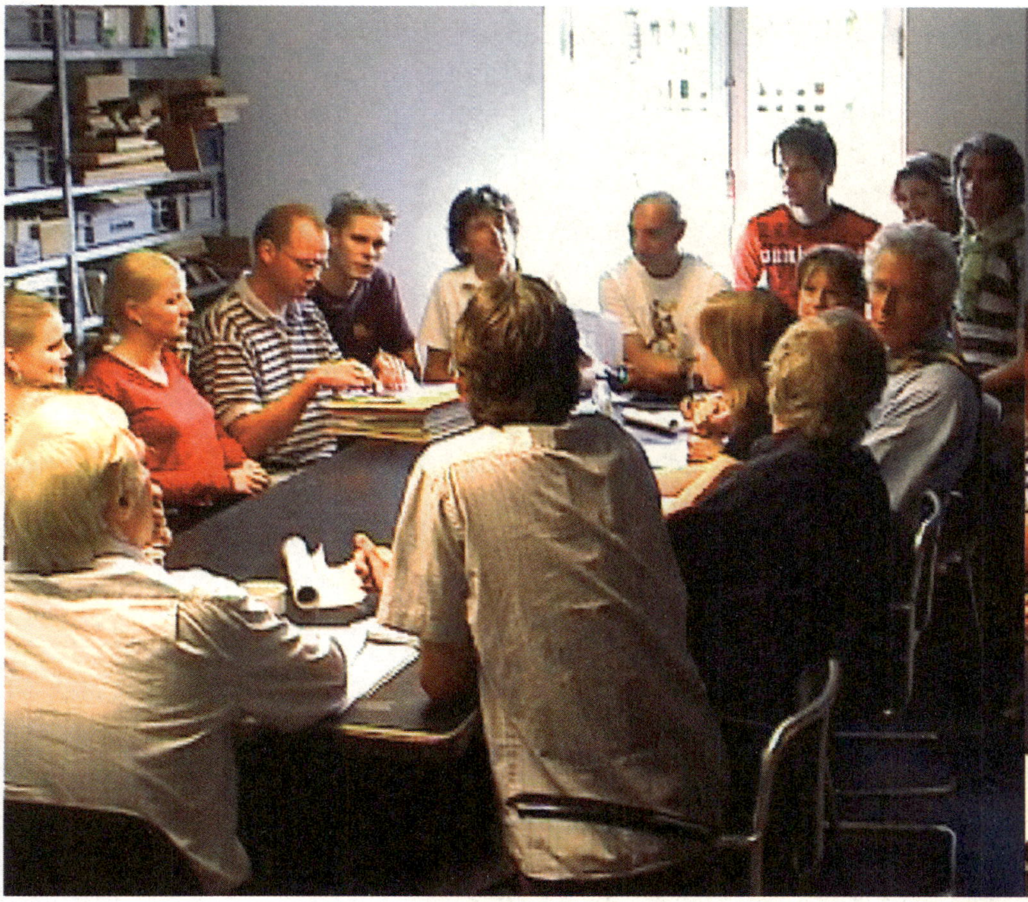
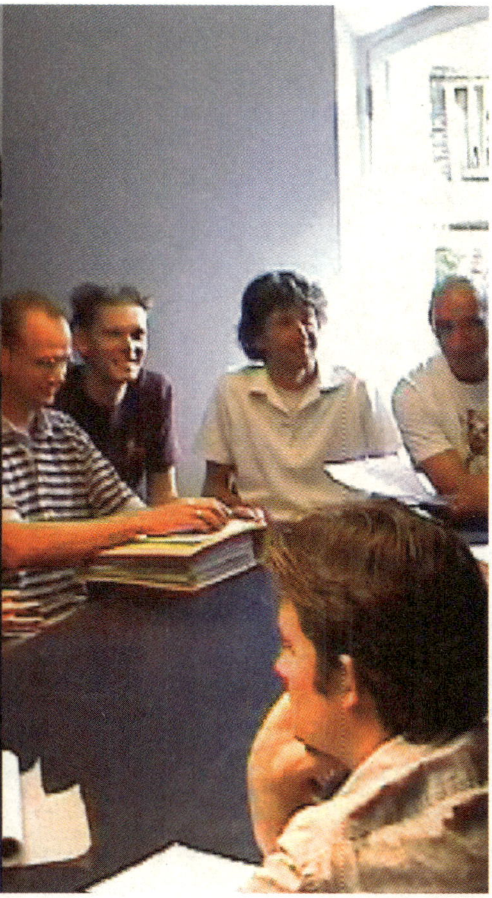
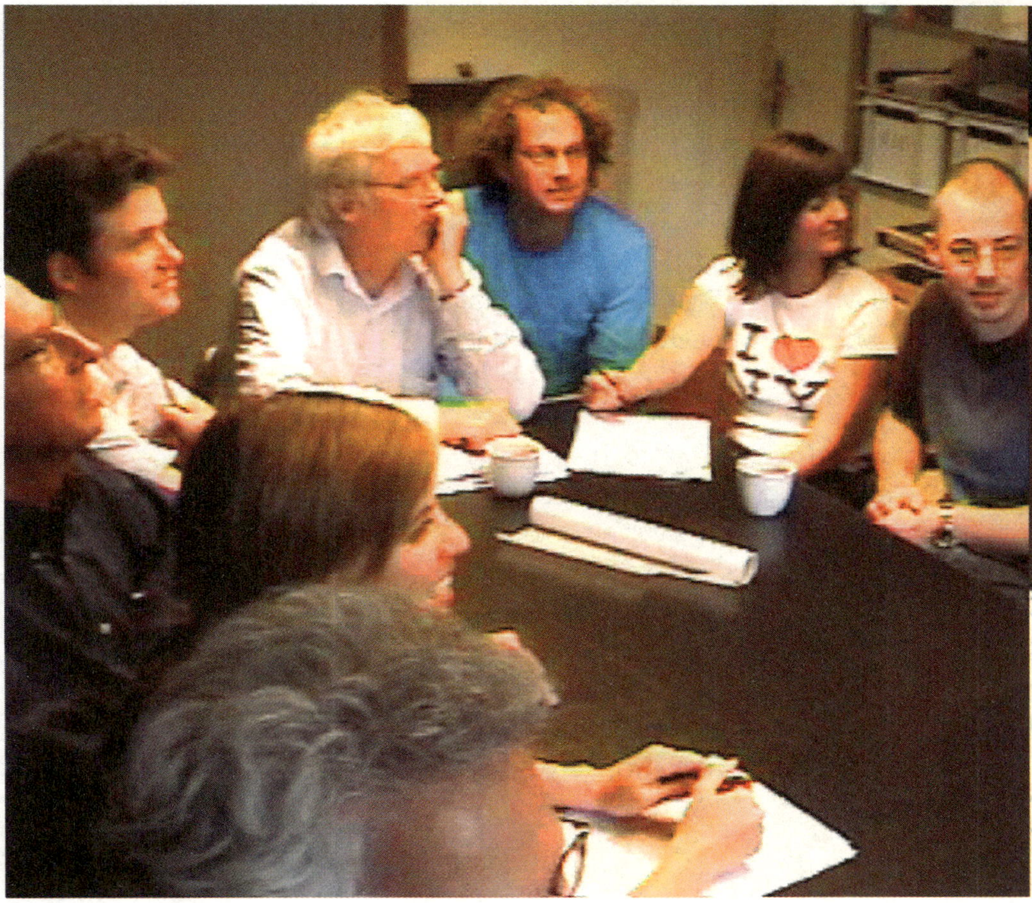
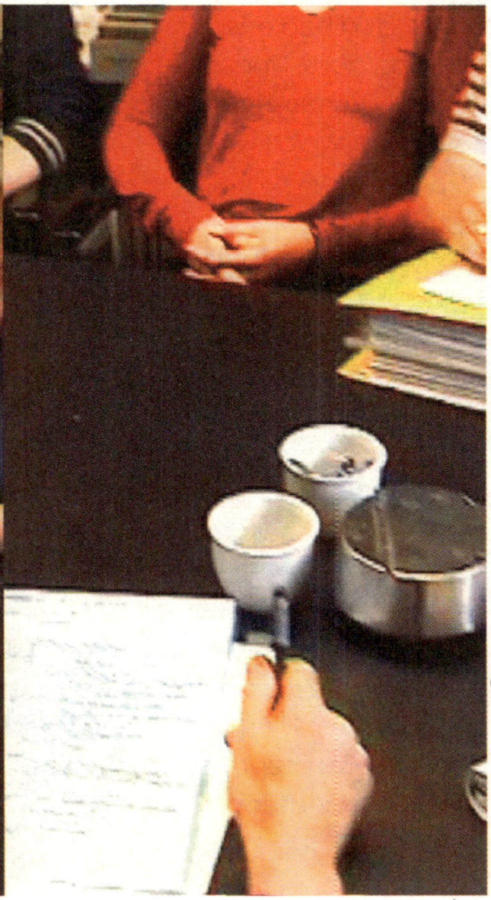

decoration is not my forte, I've plunged right in. Another example is the coach house that we're currently converting into a dwelling. The obvious choice is sturdy, bold forms. Not because I prefer such shapes, but because the space itself is begging for them.

EVELYNE MERKX

NEW START
I've practised my profession in all sorts of ways. A number of times I started all over again – new working conditions, new joint ventures, various kinds of commissions. All greatly satisfying. My first company, a joint venture with Abel Cahen, was based on symbiosis. We did everything together. A drawing left the office only if we both agreed it couldn't be better. Learned a lot, but at a certain point we'd had our fill of endless consultation. I was ready to make my own mistakes. In my next collaborative effort – this time I teamed up with Reynoud Groeneveld – the business revolved around a clear distribution of projects. Twenty years later, it was time for another change. I went into business for myself ... in a place next to Evelyne's studio. Before I knew what was happening, I was part of a new joint venture.

PATRICE GIROD

PUBLIC HOUSING
Girod-Groeneveld was involved in many public-housing projects. The early years were especially fine, thanks to ample budgets and little bureaucratic interference. I recently spoke to someone who lives in a project we built in Spaarndammerbuurt and who's very happy there. That makes me feel good. I'm proud of other projects I've worked on as well. A school in Rotterdam with upper-storey housing surely deserves a mention. As time went on, we found ourselves increasingly faced with standard commissions that required standard solutions. Today's light-hearted attitude – urban expansion projects have become much more exciting; look at the Oostelijk harbour area in Amsterdam or Rotterdam's Kop van Zuid – was hard to find in those days. Gradually I realised I'd had enough, and in 1990 I started my own business, a drastic change. Anything goes, I thought, as long as it's *not* public housing. My first commission was a block of upmarket flats on a historical square in Amsterdam. The next was De Bijenkorf in Arnhem, which was due for an addition, a renovation and new façades.

PATRICE GIROD

SELF-APPLAUSE
My strong point? That's got to be material specifications and my ability to find worthwhile solutions with relative ease. Not standard solutions but distinctive solutions that stem from careful consideration of what the client wants and needs, and of what the possibilities are. That's it.

PATRICE GIROD

Is this necessary? Let me think. My main strength is that I can crawl into the skin of a building. What does the building itself possess? What should it offer at the end of the project? I'm good at asking myself questions like these. And I'm a stylist, of course.

EVELYNE MERKX

ENTOURAGE
We were tremendously lucky to get this workplace. Just look at the light coming through those big windows. It changes every five minutes. Then there's the neighbourhood – so totally Amsterdam. I wouldn't want to be anywhere else, and certainly not in a rural environment. Mind you, I'm talking about the Netherlands. In France you've got some nice landscapes, but here . . .

PATRICE GIROD

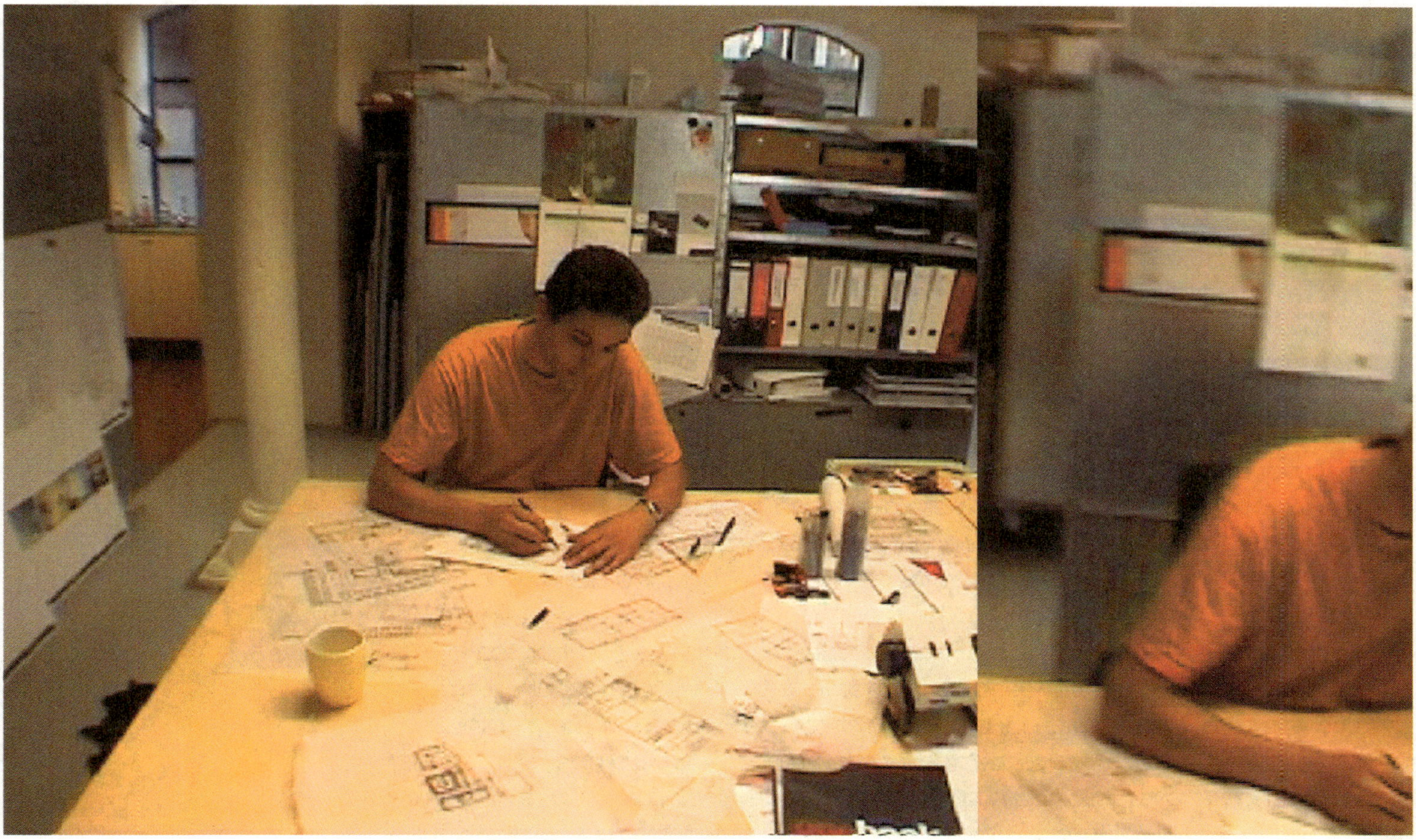

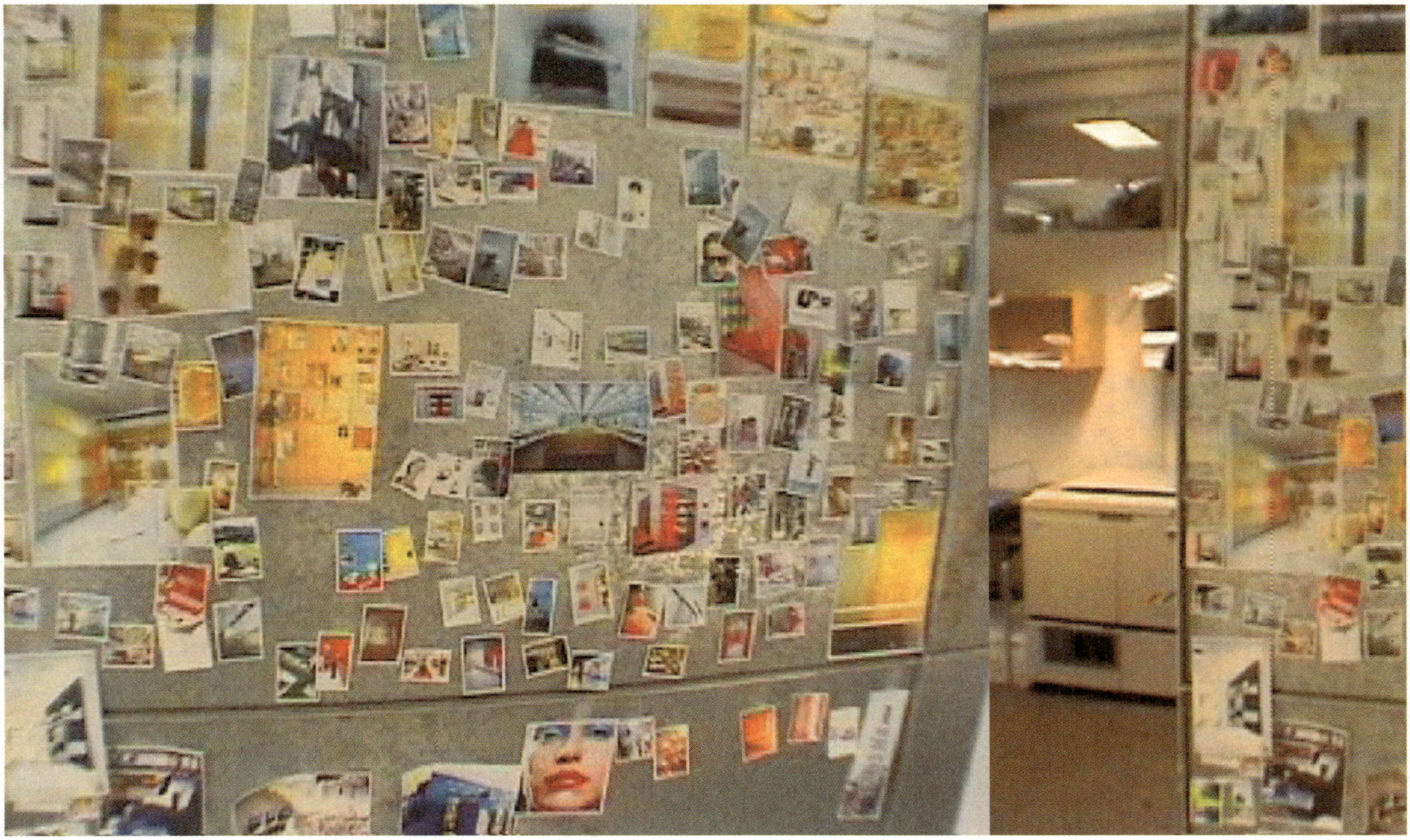

BREAKTHROUGH

At a given moment during the Girod-Groeneveld period, sitting at a desk piled high with routine work, I was asked to design a block of *upmarket* flats. Getting right to it, I came up with a powerful plan – my humble opinion then and now – in a matter of hours. That was really a breakthrough in my career, the realisation that I (still) had it in me. At the same time, I clearly saw that it was time for a change.

PATRICE GIROD

INSPIRATION

Maison de Verre, built by Pierre Chareau and Bernard Bijvoet in the thirties, is absolutely fantastic. The whole interior was created in tandem with, and especially for, the house. Brilliant. Truly beautiful. I send all my students there to look at it. A nice aspect is that the family still lives there. Because secretly that's your objective, isn't it? That people live happily ever after in the house you've designed for them.

And naturally Le Corbusier – compactness, clarity and opulence in one. Really phenomenal. Music is another source of inspiration. I feel an affinity with Schubert, for example. The way in which he repeats a theme in different ways is a quality I recognise in myself. Sometimes music helps when I'm wrestling with the balance between symmetry and asymmetry. It can help me to avoid severity and rigidity. Like the creation of a design, music is a kind of wandering. You discover one new thing after another.

I also have a great appreciation for classical architecture. Because of the eternity of refinement and beauty, of course, but the recognition factor plays a part as well. Five thousand long years ago, dedicated architects were developing solutions that differ little in essence from ours. Take the Pantheon or Versailles – yes, the architecture looks different, but apart from appearance, it all comes down to the same thing: beautiful, user-friendly buildings. A promising thought for humanity.

PATRICE GIROD

COLOUR

I always select colours intuitively, because that's how I do it. I've had a lot of practice, for that matter. For years colour prognoses were an important part of my styling consultation for De Bijenkorf.

EVELYNE MERKX

TRENDS

I'm not particularly impressed by trends. All that fanfare about so-called 'new materials' – the first time that aluminium was used convincingly in an interior was in 1905: a shop in Vienna. So... h'm...

PATRICE GIROD

Trends are fun, but they're no more than icing on the cake. Remarkable that so many people see only the sauce (colours, finishing touches, materials, a witty element perhaps) and not the radical interventions that we make in so many spaces. Interior architecture is a three-dimensional occupation. The main features are spaciousness and functionality, which must be in agreement.

EVELYNE MERKX

BLACK BOOK

12 Sure, we're faced with the occasional conflict. Companies that copy designs without letting us know, much less paying us. Clients that neglect to mention us when a design that we made for them attracts publicity. No, I won't name names. Sometimes we make a case of it; sometimes we figure it's all part of the game and simply ignore it.

EVELYNE MERKX

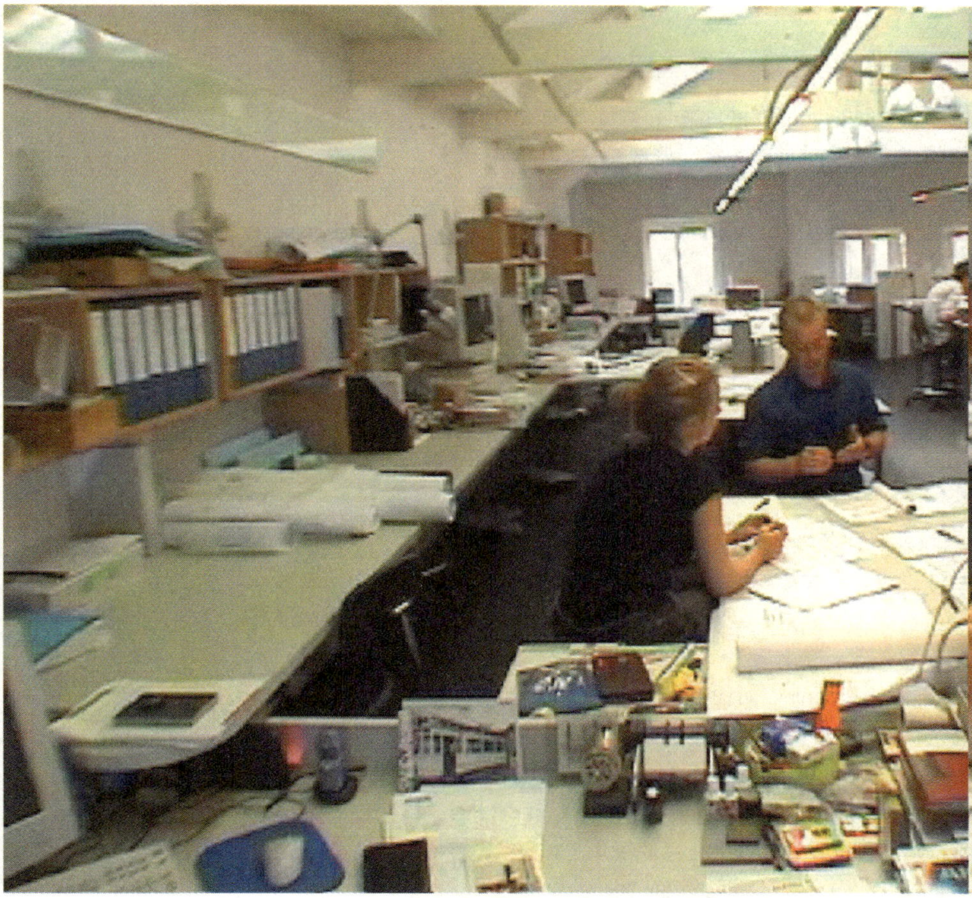
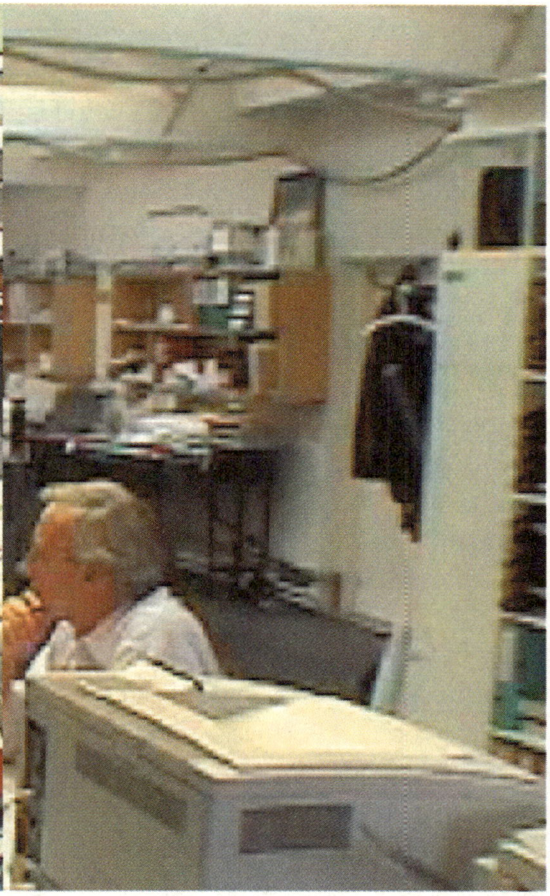
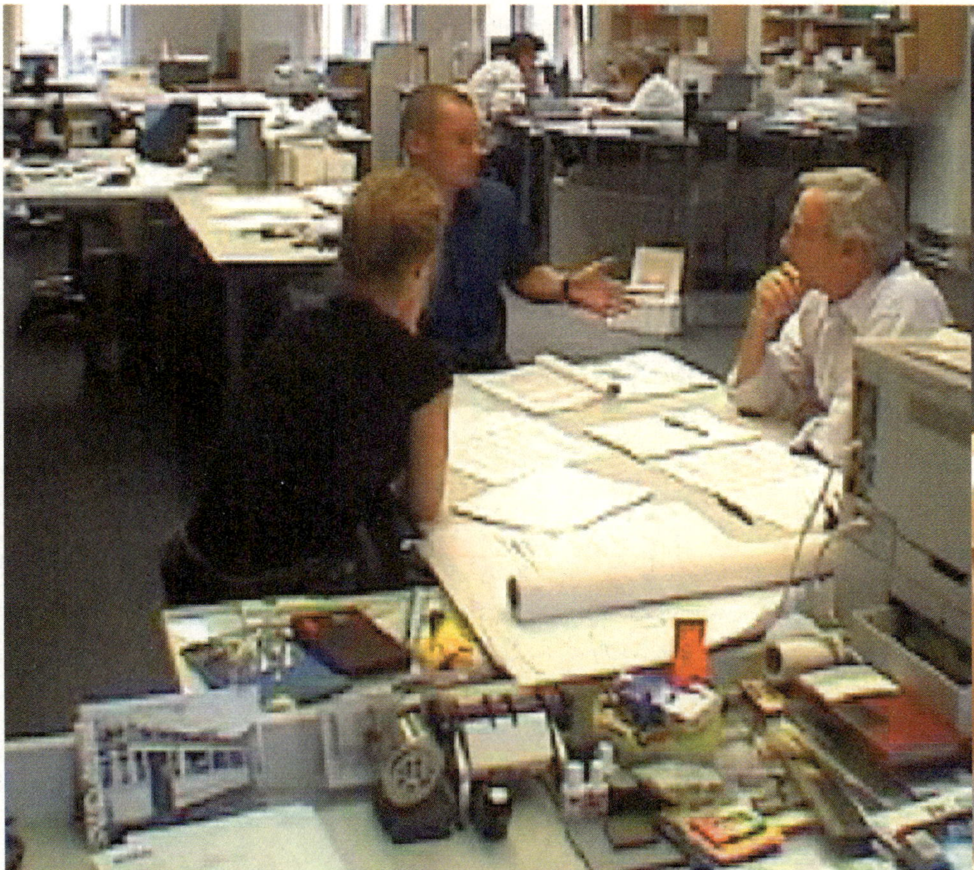
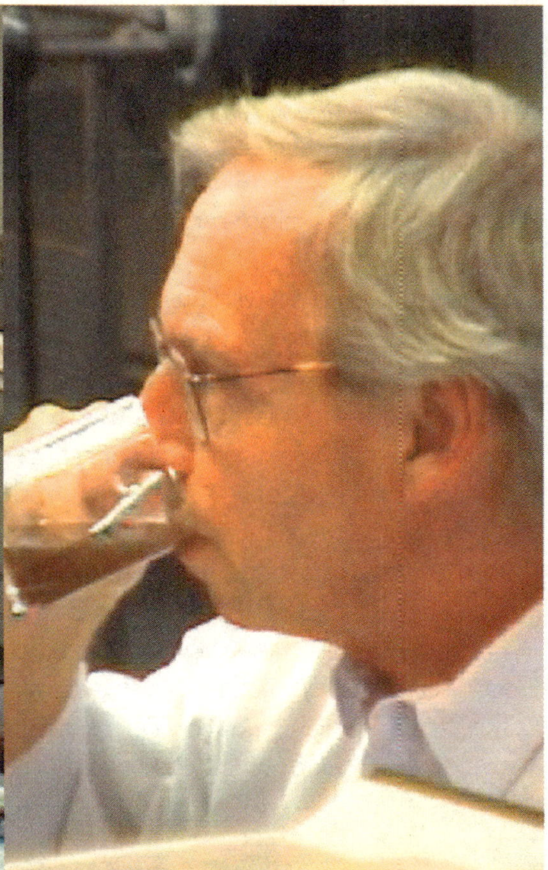

PRIVATE INTERIORS

Although beyond the scope of this book, residential designs – some very attractive homes – are part of our portfolio. Whether it's a bathroom, a kitchen or a complete interior, I love imagining myself immersed in the personal lifestyle of the occupant. But no renovation was as difficult as that of our own flat in the soap factory. Normally a smooth-working team, we now had the problem of 'two captains, one ship'.

EVELYNE MERKX

STRUCTURE

At times a firm like ours, which lacks a formal structure, can put employees/brothers-at-arms in a quandary. It's not always easy for us either. We've rejected a strict hierarchy for the sake of good teamwork. And 'cooperation' is a word that applies, thank heavens, to most of our staff.

EVELYNE MERKX

Some employees never really settle in here – they can't cope with so much independence. These people stay for a while and then leave. That's just the way it goes.

PATRICE GIROD

MUSIC

Our renovation of the Concertgebouw led to an unusual invitation. I was asked to take part in a morning-long radio programme, which was to broadcast my favourite music. The programme drew some delightful reactions, including a letter from Paul Mijksenaar. He wrote that he recognised himself to such a degree in my choice of music that he wanted me to do the renovation of his bathroom. Extraordinary. The contact between us grew into something so special that we had Paul and his wife over for dinner. Of course, table conversation included our latest project: ArboNed. Though I'd already designed quite a few graphic images for this project, I was convinced that Paul could come up with even better ideas, so I asked him to join the project. My hunch proved to be correct. The Dreyfuss book and the exercises designed to prevent RSI are absolute treasures. In the end, Mijksenaar created preventive measures, while I concentrated on remedy-related motifs.

Dutch expert in visual information systems and director of Bureau Mijksenaar.

EVELYNE MERKX

MERK X

We often design custom-made furniture – such as tables, lamps and cupboards – for our projects.
For years we've toyed with the idea of making our designs, old and new, available to a broader public under the brand name 'Merk x'. But a steady stream of commissions has left us with too little time to get the project off the ground. Recently, however, we hired people to do the job for us. We're really excited about the concept – an experimental architectonic brand that gives us an outlet for our love of design, quality and refinement.

EVELYNE MERKX

Merkx+Girod is Jeannette van den Akker, Raphaël van Amerongen, Roos Bendien, Patrick Bento, Gijs Berkhof, Klaas Cammelbeeck, Silvie Claes, Ewald Damen, Jos van Dijk, Isabelle Dollée, Sylvia van Duyvenboode, Bouwe van den Ende, Mark van der Geest, Patrice Girod, Tiemen Koetsier, Josje Kuiper, Wim van der Laan, Raymond Leentvaar, Evelyne Merkx, Bert de Munnik, Det van Oers, Geert Jan van Putten, Monique de Ridder, Marcel Steeghs, Trudy Tijs, and Jan Willem Wijker.

14

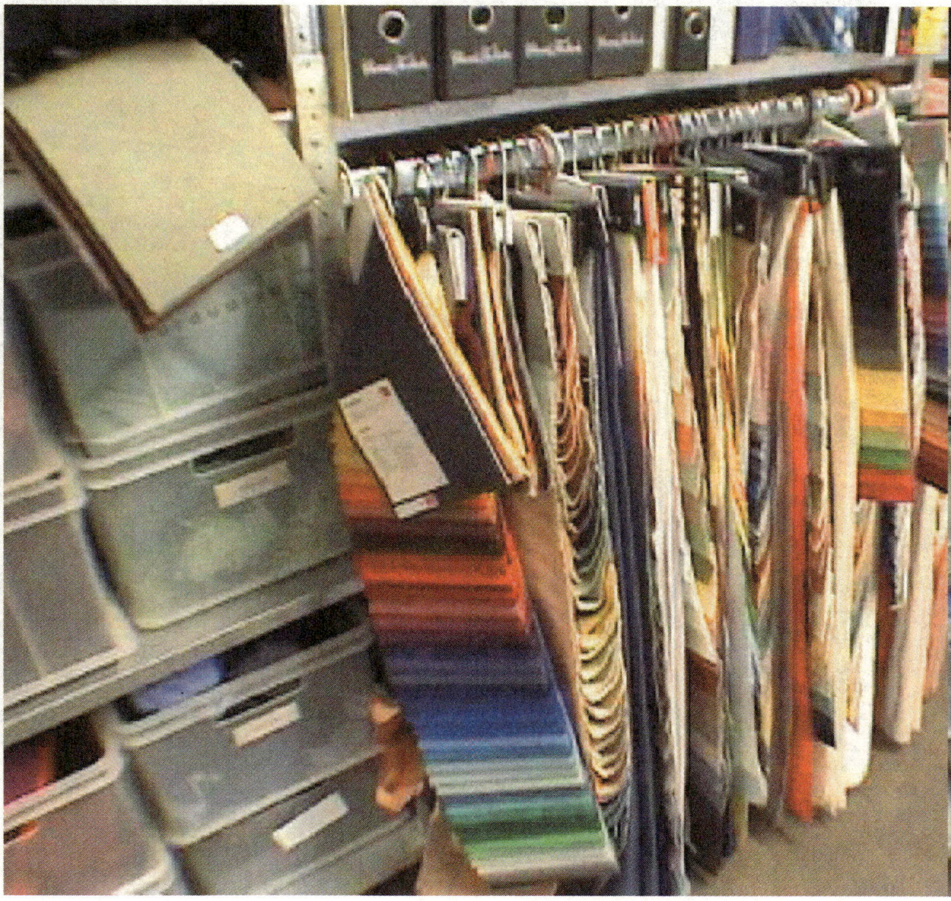
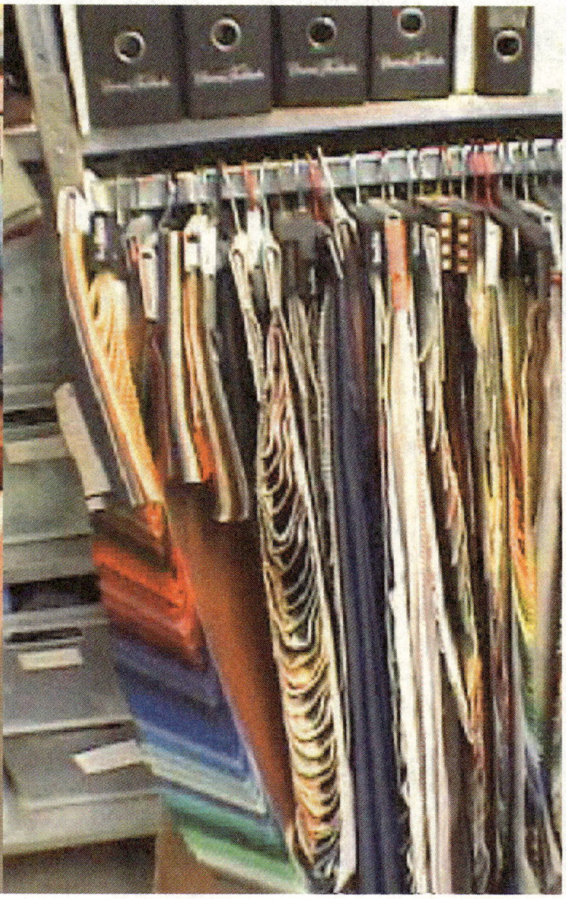
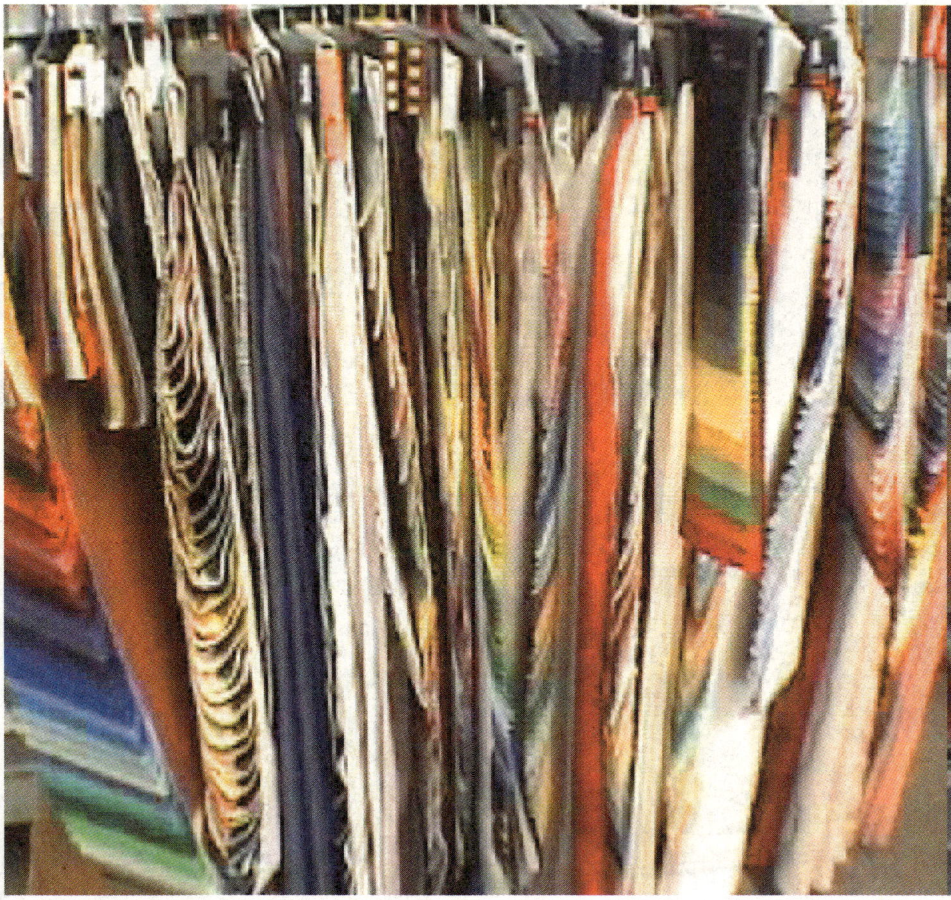
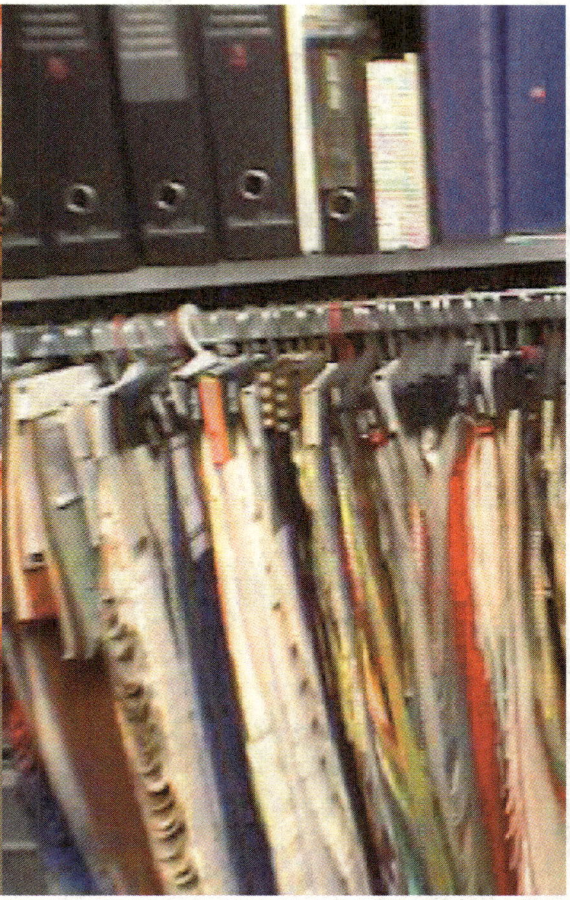

De Bijenkorf runs through our lives like a leitmotif. At the age of twenty-one I began working as a sales-promotion project manager for this big department store, a position I held until I was twenty-six – years before I entered the academy. Having just opened by own business, my first major commission was for De Bijenkorf: I provided styling consultation to those departments related to interior design and everyday surroundings. I continued doing this for fourteen years.

In 1992 we were asked to renovate the Domestic Textiles department of the Amsterdam branch of De Bijenkorf. That was the beginning of an entire series of refurbishing projects. Having completed our work in stores located in Amstelveen, Utrecht, Rotterdam, The Hague, Breda, Den Bosch and Groningen, we're currently involved in the interior design of a brand-new branch of De Bijenkorf in Maastricht.

Although the story smacks of favouritism, partiality has never played a role in our work for De Bijenkorf. I had to apply for the position of styling consultant, just like everybody else. Yes, I'd been a long-time employee of De Bijenkorf, but I'd also left that job years ago. And even after I had quite a few retail renovations under my belt, it didn't dawn on De Bijenkorf to commission me for the Amsterdam project. They did that only after I sent the board an invitation for two openings of retail spaces that I had designed (Bos Men Shop, Goes, 1989; and Van den Broek, Haarlem, 1991). Fortunately, this is a top-notch organisation and a fantastic company to work for.

DE BIJENKORF THE HAGUE, LA RUCHE RESTAURANT

'Why don't you put this restaurant in the beautiful main building that Kramer designed?' was our first question after accepting this commission. But no, the restaurant absolutely had to remain in the sombre extension added in the seventies. The biggest problem was a row of unattractive windows – twenty-four in all – that largely determined the appearance of the space. We drew the façade farther into the room by gathering window units, radiators and lighting into bays: intimate spaces accentuated by a bit of wallpaper. A reference to the somewhat fussy image of The Hague, the seat of government.

LA RUCHE, THE HAGUE 1:400
1 UNIT = 1 METER

The big felt coats are a functional feature that clearly states: Coats go here.
At the same time, they provide the large space with an eye-catching interruption.
Visitors displayed a great deal of enthusiasm for the design by 'borrowing' an
example rather all too regularly. The coats are now chained in place.

DE BIJENKORF AMSTELVEEN, LA RUCHE RESTAURANT

If the space in question is to accommodate a department-store restaurant, what do
you do with a closed rear wall, two glazed side walls and an open transition to the
Fashions department? Not to mention the difficulty posed by a kitchen that can't lie
along the exterior wall, because exhaust vents and upper-storey flats would get in
each other's way. Our solution was a centrally positioned kitchen neatly packaged in
a big glass box. An added advantage is that this volume creates – in one stroke –
a buffer between retail space and restaurant.
The use of layered glass made it possible to play with transparency. We placed photos
– our own work – between glass panels surrounding the supplies, thus shutting off the
view from one side. Diners on the side where the cooks are at work, however, have a
clear view of the activities.
From furniture to menu design, everything in this restaurant bears our signature.
René Knip assisted us with the graphics. After the project in Amstelveen, we also
renovated the restaurant in the organisation's Utrecht branch.

Zwart water vis
zilver
schaduw fijn
bliksemschicht in

Maar wat

Maar wat weet

Gerard den Brabander

De Bijenkorf The Hague, La Ruche Restaurant
Client: De Bijenkorf Department Store
Location: Wagenstraat 32, The Hague
Interior architect: Merkx+Girod Architects
Project team: Stefan Bennebroek, Mark van der Geest, Evelyne Merkx
Graphics: René Knip
Furniture: Merkx+Girod Architects, Benschop
Lighting: Merkx+Girod Architects
Floor area: 750m²
Project duration: 10 months
Completion: 2001
Photography: Roos Aldershoff

De Bijenkorf Amstelveen, La Ruche Restaurant
Client: De Bijenkorf Department Store
Location: Galerij 152, Amstelveen
Interior architect: Merkx+Girod Architects
Project team: Mark van der Geest, Patrice Girod Ina Meijer,
Evelyne Merkx
Graphics: René Knip
Lighting: Merkx+Girod Architects
Floor area: 300m²
Project duration: 1.5 years
Completion: 1998
Photography: Roos Aldershoff

DE BIJENKORF, FASHION STORES

We renovated De Bijenkorf fashion stores in Breda, Den Bosch and Groningen and gave them brand-new interiors in the bargain. These outlets, which are considerably smaller that their big-city sisters, are devoted chiefly to clothing, supplemented by a number of concepts involving food and restaurant facilities and an element featuring home furnishings. A small-scale department store. The challenge was to make optimum use of the relatively limited space and, at the same time, to preserve surveyability, transparency and clarity. All that within eight months. The façades of these stores were part of the project.

De Bijenkorf, Fashion Stores
Client: De Bijenkorf Department Store
Location: Karrestraat 24-26, Breda
Interior architect: Merkx+Girod Architects
Project team: Raphaël van Amerongen, Ewald Damen, Mark van der Geest, Patrice Girod, Evelyne Merkx, Rupert Swirn (Aswa Architects)
Graphics: René Knip, M3
Furniture: Merkx+Girod Architects, Benschop
Floor area: 3400m²
Project duration: 8 months
Completion: 2001
Photography: Roos Aldershoff

DE BIJENKORF AMSTELVEEN, 1:400
1 UNIT = 1 METER

DE BIJENKORF AMSTELVEEN, HOME FURNISHINGS AND MEDIA DEPARTMENTS

We shared this commission with London firm Virgile & Stone. Together we developed a plan of approach and the routing that emerged from this plan. They designed the ground and first floors; we were responsible for the basement. Here, too, we designed all the furniture. Simple, elegant and hooligan-proof.

In response to the relatively small floor space, we collaborated with in-house project groups to create a new retail concept for this department store. Products bearing a relationship to one another were grouped in so-called 'worlds': pans, espresso cups, varieties of fresh pasta and cookery books, for example, shared the same display space.

We also developed a special system for the book department: a sturdy, centrally positioned display element that remains flexible even while supporting a great deal of weight. Here the language of form follows the same pattern seen in previously designed furniture for the Cookery department at De Bijenkorf in Amsterdam.

In designing the gigantic, freestanding, orange and yellow wall with display niches, which is located next to the escalators, we tried to forge two floors into a single visual entity, while also indicating where customers can find the Home Furnishings department.

De Bijenkorf Amstelveen, Home Furnishings and Media departments
Client: De Bijenkorf Department Store
Location: Galerij 152, Amstelveen
Interior architect: Merkx+Girod Architects
Project team: Mark van der Geest, Olaf Kramer, Evelyne Merkx, Jan Willem Wijker
Graphics: René Knip
Furniture: Merkx+Girod Architects, Benschop
Floor area: 2000m²
Project duration: 1 year
Completion: 1998
Photography: Alexander van Berge

DE BIJENKORF AMSTERDAM, DOMESTIC TEXTILES DEPARTMENT
(CURTAINS, BED LINEN, TOWELS AND SO FORTH)

Even today, I'm proud of having liberated the windows, which had been barricaded and used for wall displays. All department stores followed this strategy in those days – every square metre counts. But I wanted light and air. The argument that settled the issue was: People don't sit in the dark at home either.

We didn't design display tables and racks without giving the matter any thought. We did a tremendous amount of research into the activities of this department. The table we designed for measuring material, for example, features a lowered channel that holds the roll of fabric and, by means of a built-in motor, allows the salesperson to unwind the material without having to lift the heavy roll. We also created what has come to be known as a 'mimi-set': three display tables that fit into one another. The client liked our design for the Domestic Textiles department of the Amsterdam Bijenkorf so much that it went on to serve as a model for comparable departments in other branches of De Bijenkorf.

The purpose-built furniture – robust tables with stainless-steel feet, for example, a *highly* imitated design – remains unchanged, twelve years later. Every new branch of De Bijenkorf gets its own copy of the Domestic Textiles department that first appeared in Amsterdam in 1993.

De Bijenkorf Amsterdam, Domestic Textiles Department
Client: De Bijenkorf Department Store
Location: Dam 1, Amsterdam
Interior architect: Studio Merkx
Project team: Josje Kuiper, Evelyne Merkx, Jan Willem Wijker
Furniture: Merkx+Girod Architects, Benschop
Project duration: 1 year
Completion: 1993
Photography: Roos Aldershoff

DE BIJENKORF, COOKERY SHOPS

We took the same approach to the Cookery Shop that we had taken to the adjacent Domestic Textiles department. All furnishings are our own designs. A freestanding shelving system of steel and wood, for example, bears the weight of heavy kitchen appliances without complaint. We developed all graphic-design elements in collaboration with René Knip.

De Bijenkorf, Cookery Shops
Client: De Bijenkorf Department Store
Location: Dam 1, Amsterdam
Interior architect: Studio Merkx
Project team: Josje Kuiper, Evelyne Merkx, Jan Willem Wijker
Graphics: René Knip
Furniture: Merkx+Girod Architects, Benschop
Project duration: 8 months
Completion: 1996
Photography: Pieter Vlamings

DE BIJENKORF ARNHEM

After leaving Girod-Groeneveld Architects to set up my own business, one of the first jobs I did as Patrice Girod was De Bijenkorf in Arnhem. A whacking great commission. Renovated in the fifties, the department store resembled the beehive whose name it bore (*bijenkorf* is Dutch for 'beehive'). A small, low entrance led to an enormous volume crisscrossed by narrow aisles and suffocating from a lack of natural light. The main intervention, therefore, involved inviting daylight into the building. One way was to open the roof above the escalators. Another was to leave a gap between the existing store and a new-build volume at the rear, a decision that resulted in a light shaft, complete with footbridges.

Terrific project. Good clients – real department-store fanatics, with an interest in matters above and beyond the number of square metres of retail (read 'sales') space. I had no problem exchanging ideas with them on what I saw as the big challenge of the project. The main entrance of the building faces a busy shopping street, while the rear façade of the new-build extension is part of a quiet, small-scale, inner-city neighbourhood. Thus the main façade needed to radiate a cosmopolitan character (the store attracts both Dutch and German customers), and the rear exterior required a more subdued look. Despite the dichotomy, however, the store had to present itself as a unified volume.

This story has an unexpected ending. It wasn't Evelyne who did the interior – although we had an intensive working relationship at that point, we hadn't yet merged our companies – but the English firm Virgile & Stone, an outfit that had done a lot of work for the department store. De Bijenkorf distributes its favours a bit.

DE BIJENKORF MAASTRICHT

Our most recent project for the organisation. And one of the biggest yet. We've been asked to design the complete interior.

De Bijenkorf Arnhem
Client: De Bijenkorf Department Store
Location: Ketelstraat 45, Arnhem
Architect: Patrice Girod
Project team: Patrice Girod, Gerrit Kuen, Josje Kuiper, Wim van der Laan
Interior architects: De Bijenkorf In-House Design Team, Patrice Girod, Virgile & Stone London
Project duration: 3 years
Completion: 1994
Photography: Robert Sledziewski

VAN GOGH MUSEUM SHOP, AMSTERDAM

VAN GOGH MUSEUM SHOP AND PAVILION

SHOP

Designed by Gerrit Rietveld, the Van Gogh Museum experienced a radical renovation in 1999. The lion's share of the work was done by Dutch firm Greiner and Goor and Japanese architect Kisho Kurokawa. We were asked to design the museum shop. Our involvement was actually a special request made by Mrs Cramer-Van Gogh, the granddaughter of Vincent van Gogh's beloved brother Theo.

In an earlier renovation plan, the office was located at one of the most attractive places in the building: the spot that now accommodates the shop. The focus of our approach was the removal of this enclosed block and the liberation of five tall, magnificent windows. We felt that storage and administrative areas didn't belong in the shop itself, so we designed an entresol that extends the length of the adjacent cloakroom – an element that leaves the window behind it as free as possible, of course. For the flooring, we took our cue from the slate surface in the adjoining hall. Rather than using rough blocks, however, we laid the slate in strips polished to a sheen. It looks like a pinstripe suit. Chandeliers featuring T-bulbs are a Merkx+Girod design.

PAVILION

Placing a shop within a largely transparent pavilion is not an easy task. We solved the problem of a potential lack of display space – a threat to the transparent quality we were so keen to preserve – by installing a double skin. Shelves in front of the windows are interrupted by openings that face both street and retail space, allowing the two sides to be used for displaying merchandise.

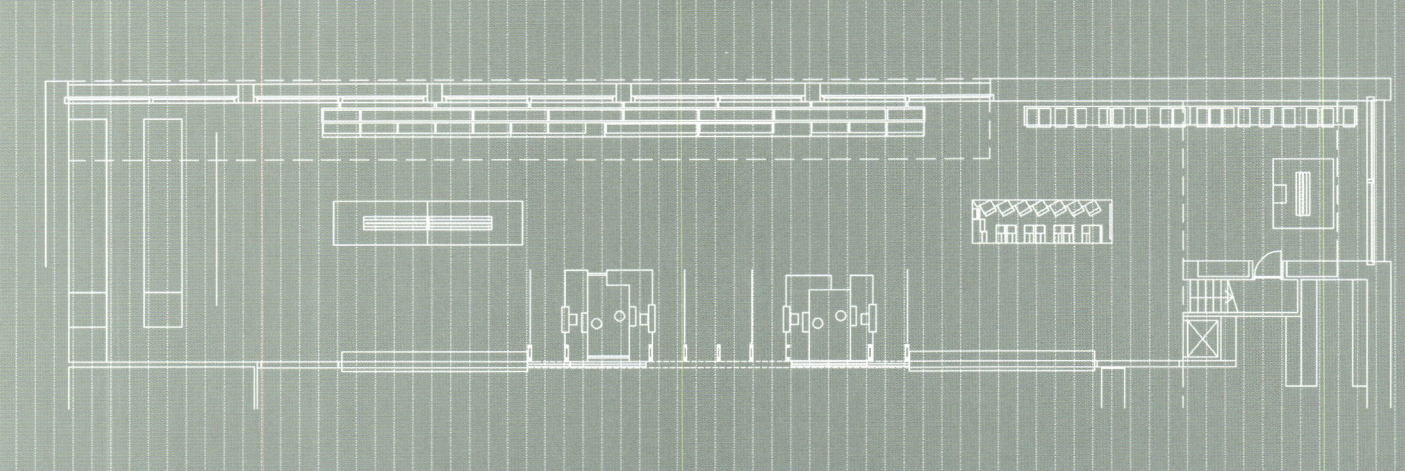

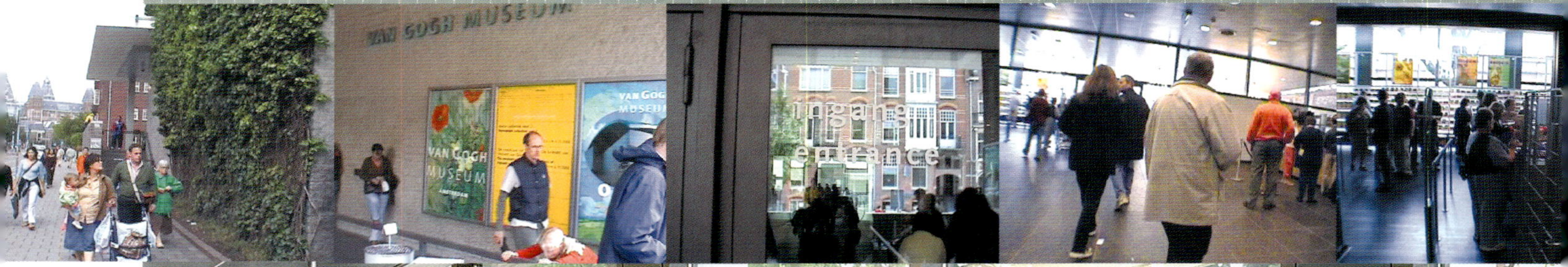

VAN GOGH MUSEUM SHOP, AMSTERDAM, 1:200
2 UNITS = 1 METER

VAN GOGH MUSEUM

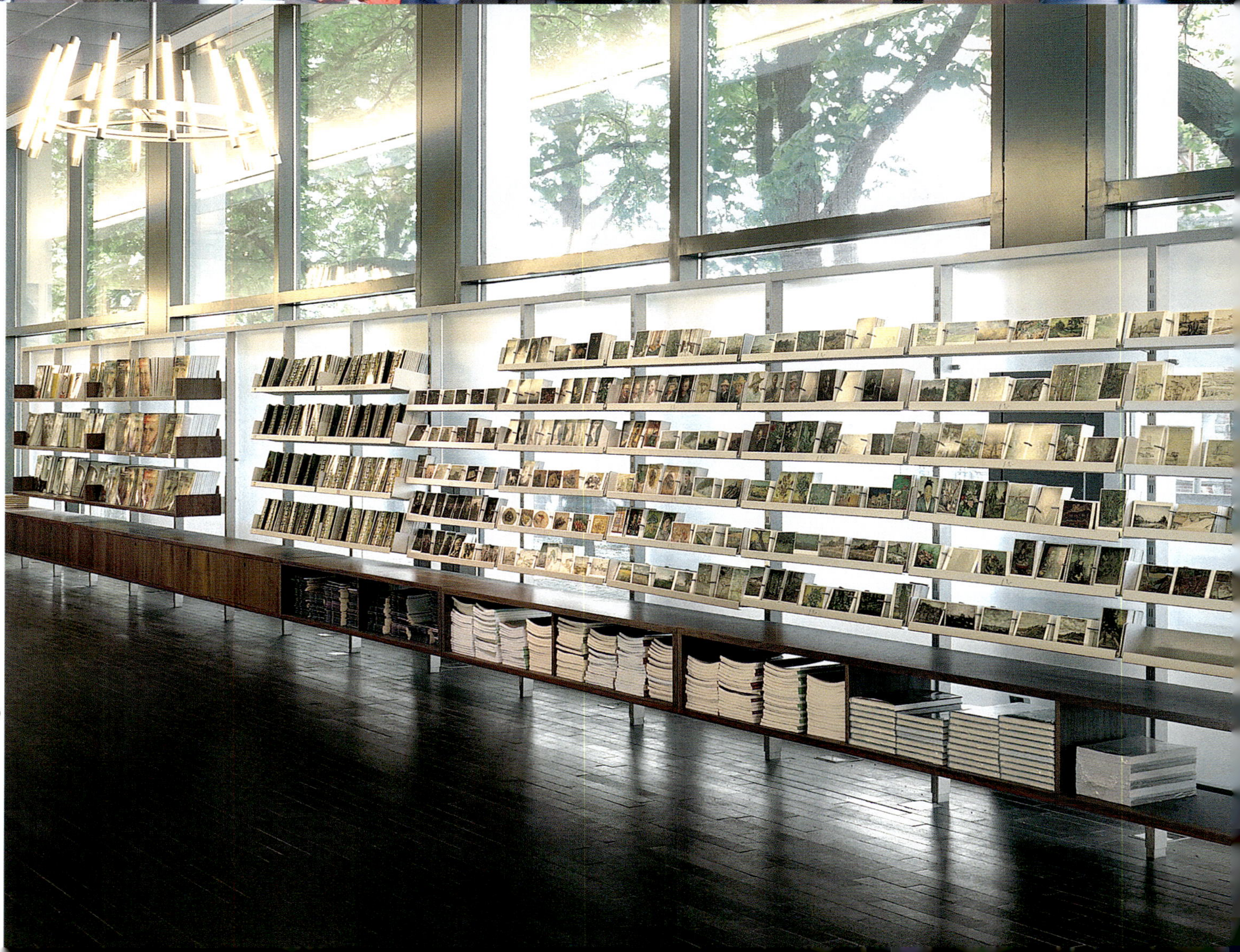

39

Van Gogh Museum Shop
Client: 't Landhuys, Mrs T.Cramer-Van Gogh
Location: Paulus Potterstraat 7, Amsterdam
Interior architect: Merkx+Girod Architects
Project team: Stefan Bennebroek, Ewald Damen, Evelyne Merkx,
Jan Willem Wijker
Furniture: Merkx+Girod Architects, Benschop
Lighting: Merkx+Girod Architects, Robin Hood Productions
Floor area: 375m²
Project duration: 1 year
Completion: 1999
Photography: Roos Aldershoff

41

Van Gogh Museum Pavilion
Client: Van Gogh Museum, in cooperation with the Rijksmuseum
Location: Museumplein, Amsterdam
Interior architect: Merkx+Girod Architects
Project team: Ina Meijer, Evelyne Merkx, Jan Willem Wijker
Furniture: Merkx+Girod Architects, Benschop
Lighting: Merkx+Girod Architects
Project duration: 6 months
Completion: 1999
Photography: Roos Aldershoff

ANNA VAN TOOR, THE HAGUE, 1:200
GROUND FLOOR
2 UNITS = 1 METER

ANNA VAN TOOR

How do you transform a chain of fashion shops? The imaginary name 'Anna van Toor'
was and is – the project is ongoing – the basis of our design. Anna van Toor is the
metaphor for a rather headstrong woman, a figure not without mystique. Retail image,
packaging materials and typography, a task efficiently handled by René Knip: for once
the term 'a complete transformation' is not an empty phrase. More recently
we initiated a line of womenswear called 'Anna', a brand with modelling books
provided by M3*.

Anna van Toor couples elegance with a preference for a natural, no-fuss look. With
this personality in mind, we used a delicate floral motif for the walls, selected
flooring of panga panga wood and crafted fitting rooms of thick felt. Four shops have
been completed: in Breda, The Hague, Utrecht and Tiel. Plans are to transform about
14 additional outlets.

*Partnership of designers Marty Lammers, Shirley
Muijrers and Evelyne Merkx in product development,
interior textiles and styling.

Anna van Toor The Hague
Client: Van Toor Fashion
Location: Hoogstraat 29, The Hague
Interior architect: Merkx+Girod Architects
Project team: Patrice Girod, Wim van der Laan, Evelyne Merkx
Graphic design: Merkx+Girod Architects, René Knip
Furniture: Merkx+Girod Architects, WSB Interieurbouw
Floor area: 400m²
Project duration: 5 months
Completion: 2001
Photography: Roos Aldershoff

Anna van Toor Breda
Client: Van Toor Fashion
Location: Karrestraat 13, Breda
Interior architect: Merkx+Girod Architects
Project team: Wim van der Laan, Evelyne Merkx
Graphic design: Merkx+Girod Architects, René Knip
Furniture: Merkx+Girod Architects, WSB Interieurbouw
Floor area: 400m²
Project duration: 8 months
Completion: 2000
Photography: Lajos Geenen

GRAND CAFÉ RESTAURANT

My first public-works project was a commission I realised in collaboration
with Jan Marc van Eendenburg: the conversion of a badly neglected space on
Platform 2b of Cuypers's railway station in Amsterdam into a café-restaurant.
All good elements were to be preserved – lavishly painted ceilings, a carved
buffet and wooden wainscoting, for example – and the rest replaced. Right down
to the details. One of our creations was what we called 'glow-worms': perforated
steel screens backed by tiny lamps. Another was an adaptation of a lamp designed
by Josef Hoffmann, which we provided with a new pendant. We reserved a place of
honour for a vase from the collection of the Queen, who has her own waiting room
on this platform. We asked Anthon Beeke to design the logo.
All that was 17 years ago, and visitors are still enjoying the same interior.

51

Grand Café Restaurant
Client: Maarten van den Biggelaar
Location: Platform 2b, Amsterdam Central Station
Interior architects: Jan Marc van Eendenburg, Evelyne Merkx
Graphics: Anthon Beeke
Project duration: 9 months
Completion: 1986
Photography: Roos Aldershoff

ABN AMRO BANK, AMSTERDAM

ABN AMRO BANK

Pei Cobb Freed & Partners, an American firm who designed new headquarters for the ABN Amro Bank on Amsterdam's explosively growing South Axis, has, in the words of Patrice Girod, 'an explicit preference for stately proposals'. Looking for a counterbalance to that quality, the bank's board of directors thought of Merkx+Girod.

Staking out our territory while our colleagues staked out theirs turned into an endless tug-of-war, with fortnightly meetings in Amsterdam or New York. The American outfit claimed the entrance, the dealing room and the conference hall. The rest, which still covered a good four-fifths of the interior (a total of 90,000 square metres), was yielded to 'the Amsterdammers'.

Our first concern was to allow natural light to penetrate the colossal building as deeply as possible. We broke out stairwells, inserted entresols and footbridges, and managed to add voids that rise through several levels. Stairs placed within these voids create vertical connections that break the monotony of never-ending corridors and serve as a time-saving device by reducing the distance that employees have to walk. An added advantage is an abundance of vertical surfaces large enough to accommodate sizable works of art. We had a fight on our hands when it came to plans for restaurants and service points. In the end it was 'win some, lose some'.

Furniture is a separate story. Because everybody involved – masses of people in a big headquarters like this one – had a say in the choice of office furniture, we decided to make an exhibition of the options. Having picked the colours and materials desired, we asked a selection of suppliers to submit their merchandise. We designed a neutral arrangement of the pieces in an empty office building and invited everybody to view, test and vote on the furniture. Visitors filled in questionnaires and used a point system to evaluate the various items. Two years later the winner was announced, and the order went out for truckloads of furniture.

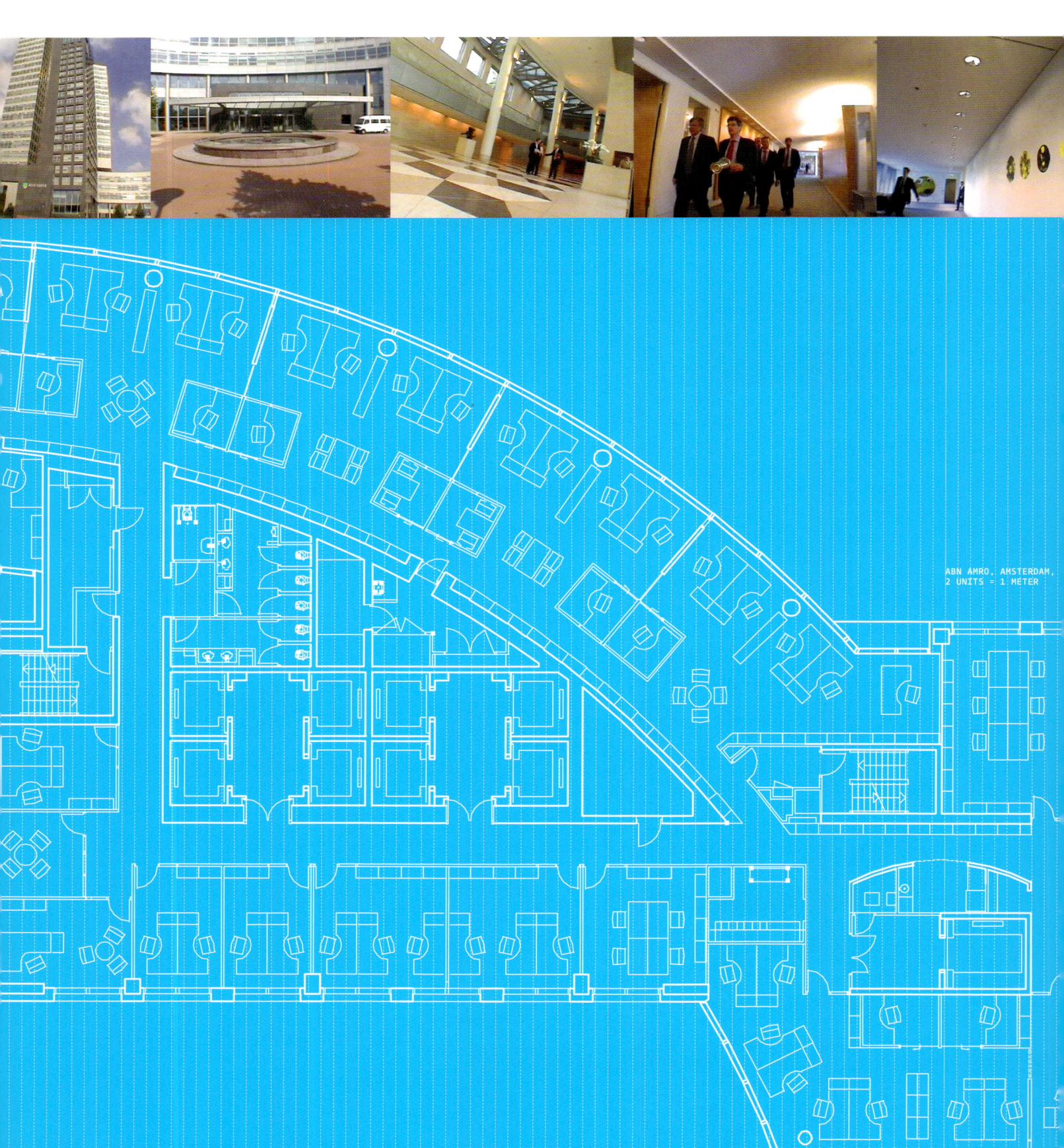

ABN AMRO, AMSTERDAM,
2 UNITS = 1 METER

ABN AMRO Bank
Client: ABN AMRO
Location: Amsterdam Buitenveldert
Architect: Pei Cobb Freed & Partners, New York
Interior architect: Merkx+Girod Architects (35 service points,
2 in-house restaurants and 3200 workstations)
Project team: Mark van der Geest, Patrice Girod, Josje Kuiper,
Wim van der Laan, Evelyne Merkx
Office furnishings: Ahrend (desks), Wilkhahn (chairs),
Lensvelt (cabinets), Philips (lighting), Bruynzeel, Saint Roche,
Unifor (partition walls), Günter Forg (art displayed in voids)
In-house-restaurant furnishings: Acaba (chairs), Wilkhahn (tables),
Merkx+Girod Architects (lighting)

Floor area: 90,000m²
Project duration: 5 years
Completion: 1999
Photography: Roos Aldershoff

YPERLAAN / VAN DEN BROEK PHOTO STUDIO

Stunning photo studio. The clients haven't changed a thing. They needed an area for shooting photos that could be completely darkened. As a counterbalance to the austere white floor of cast-in-place concrete, I opted for lofty wooden shutters. A peephole allows those in the office to see what's happening in the studio. We addressed the need for office space in such tight quarters by providing the plan with an intermediate level. The purpose-designed spiral staircase of cast aluminium features a lacy pattern on the treads – a rather frivolous touch in this sober interior. A whim I just couldn't ignore.

Yperlaan / Van den Broek Photo Studio
Clients: Annemarieke van den Broek, Ernst Yperlaan
Location: Passeerdersgracht 17, Amsterdam
Interior architect: Studio Merkx
Project team: Evelyne Merkx
General contractor: Van den Hengel
Project duration: 1 year
Completion: 1989
Photography: Annemarieke van den Broek

PMS v W/YOUNG & RUBICAM

An important feature of our plan for the reception area of this ad agency was
a counter clad in silver leaf. But no matter how many experts we consulted, we
couldn't make it happen. The counter was intolerably vulnerable to damage. We
were forced to use red lead and to insist, in a chant around the edge, that 'this
is silver leaf … this is silver leaf … this is silver leaf …' The line on the
floor leads straight to the lift. Visitors with time to spare can stop at the
curving wall, where slide viewers offer examples of the agency's ad campaigns.
Little winged lamps (Ingo Maurer) on this sky-blue wall refer to the KLM swans,
a PMS v W/Young & Rubicam brainchild. Post goes in canvas mailbags, keys are
kept behind a king-size keyhole, and heavy sliding doors confine not prisoners,
but printers.

PMS v W/Young & Rubicam
Client: PMS v W/Young & Rubicam
Location: Frans van Mierisstraat 92, Amsterdam
Interior architect: Studio Merkx
Project team: Josje Kuiper, Evelyne Merkx, Jan Willem Wijker
Floor area: 100m²
Project duration: 8 months
Completion: 1994
Photography: Robert Sledziewski

MARCCAIN

To get the maximum use from a space, a void is sometimes *the* solution. Especially if you position the floor to receive daylight from the side, as well as from above and below. When I designed this particular void, I'd had next to no experience in construction. Colleague Jan Willem Wijker and I sweat blood trying to get it right; with the support of 'our Frenchman' Patrice, however, we did manage to complete the task. Besides the retail floor of the womenswear shop, the project also included an upstairs office and several flats. The only thing that remained unchanged was the façade. The mezzanine, the void, the footbridge to the terrace, the lighting system and all furnishings were designed especially for this project. The pattern on the entrance doors (wood and coloured glass in yellow, green and pink) is based on the letters in the brand name Marccain. I can still picture myself lying on the floor, endlessly shifting shapes cut from cardboard.

Marccain
Client: Röling Import
Location: Rue J. Stas 8, Brussels, Belgium
Interior architect: Studio Merkx
Project team: Patrice Girod, Josje Kuiper, Evelyne Merkx, Jan Willem Wijker
Project duration: 1.5 years
Completion: 1991
Photography: Roos Aldershoff

RÖLING IMPORT

Standing in the hall, the visitor gets a foretaste of what's about to unfold in the basement showroom. Not a bolt from the blue, but a diffuse suggesticn. The pattern on the etched glass is based on an actual lace-making motif.

Röling Import
Client: Röling Import
Location: Zuidermolenweg 2, Amsterdam
Interior architect: Studio Merkx
Project team: Josje Kuiper, Evelyne Merkx
Project duration: 6 months
Completion: 1992
Photography: Pieter Vlamings

LIDEWIJ EDELKOORT TRADE-FAIR STAND

In 1992 Lidewij Edelkoort had the opportunity to show her work at Heimtex (*the* trade fair for domestic textiles) in a 10-metre-high building scheduled for demolition. Fantastic. To get a grip on the gigantic space, Branko Vlamings and I designed huge boxes made of container wood. Marijke Griffioen created the enormous stamps. A fair is like the theatre – it's about effect, not eternity. Clouds of light were produced by 1100 (!) simple light bulbs hanging on equally simple flexes.

Lidewij Edelkoort Trade-Fair Stand
Client: Lidewij Edelkoort
Location: Heimtextil, Frankfurt, Germany
Interior architect: Studio Merkx
Project team: Evelyne Merkx, Branko Vlamings
Graphics: Marijke Griffioen
Project duration: 6 months
Completion: 1992
Photography: Studio Edelkoort

KENNEDY VAN DER LAAN

In anticipation of permanent quarters, which won't be completed for a couple of years, this law firm is temporarily housed in a new but nondescript office building. The lawyers want a workplace whose young, dynamic image equals that of the firm. Their provisional office provides us with an opportunity to test a number of ideas and solutions for the permanent situation. We're looking at how to combine closed and open office plans, how to evoke the suggestion of a doorless space, how to simplify the use of materials to a bare minimum while retaining a sense of allure and so forth.

Kennedy van der Laan
Client: Kennedy van der Laan
Location: Haarlemmerweg 333, Amsterdam
Interior architect: Merkx+Girod Architects
Project team: Patrice Girod, Evelyne Merkx, Trudy Tijs,
Hans Tomassen (Aswa Architects), Jan Willem Wijker,
Furniture: Merkx+Girod Architects, Keijsers Interior Projects
Project duration: 1.5 years
Completion: 2002
Photography: Lajos Geenen

CAPI LUX IMAGE FACTORY I

A decade ago Capi Lux invited recently graduated photographers and technicians to test the latest innovations in this experimental workspace. Our job was to design a suitable environment.

We outfitted the harbour warehouse in Amsterdam with a black asphalt floor and soundproof wooden containers. A flexible space for activities was the number-one priority, but it seemed only logical to provide this happening with movable furniture. The wheeled computer table is our own design.

CAPI LUX IMAGE FACTORY II

When the time came to expand its successful formula, Capi Lux called on us to participate in the project. Dripping to the floor from the coffee container we designed was a pool of milk – a joke, of course, but also a reference to Dutch artist Klaas Gubbels, known around the world for his oversized coffeepots.

Capi Lux Image Factory I / II
Client: Martin Breuer
Location: Basisweg 42, Amsterdam
Interior architect: Studio Merkx
Project team: Patrice Girod, Josje Kuiper, Evelyne Merkx,
Branko Vlamings, Jan Willem Wijker
Graphics: Anthon Beeke
Floor area: 600m²
Project duration: 1 year (1993), 6 months (1996)
Completion: 1993, 1996
Photography: Pieter Vlamings

DE INKTPOT, UTRECHT

DE INKTPOT ('THE INKWELL')

The 22 million bricks that make this building the largest brick structure in the Netherlands once displayed a palette of lighter shades. Down through the years, however, the office building gradually changed into a glowering bunker. The interior of the colossus built by architect Van Heukelom of Dutch Railways (still the owner of the building) made an equally sombre, and dilapidated impression. Van Stigt Architects took charge of the exterior renovation, while the interior was a Merkx+Girod project. Another battle for power. We're not against the preservation of original materials, but we also see nothing wrong with incorporating a contemporary addition now and again.

A major problem was the wiring. Brickwork all over the interior prevented us from installing wiring in the walls. The solution lay in a 40-mm-thick raised floor on the existing tile floor, creating a raceway running throughout the building. Wiring and floor lamps are incorporated into this element. By placing it free of the walls, we kept the original details of the floor tiles intact. Not only a practical solution, but also a strong visual element.

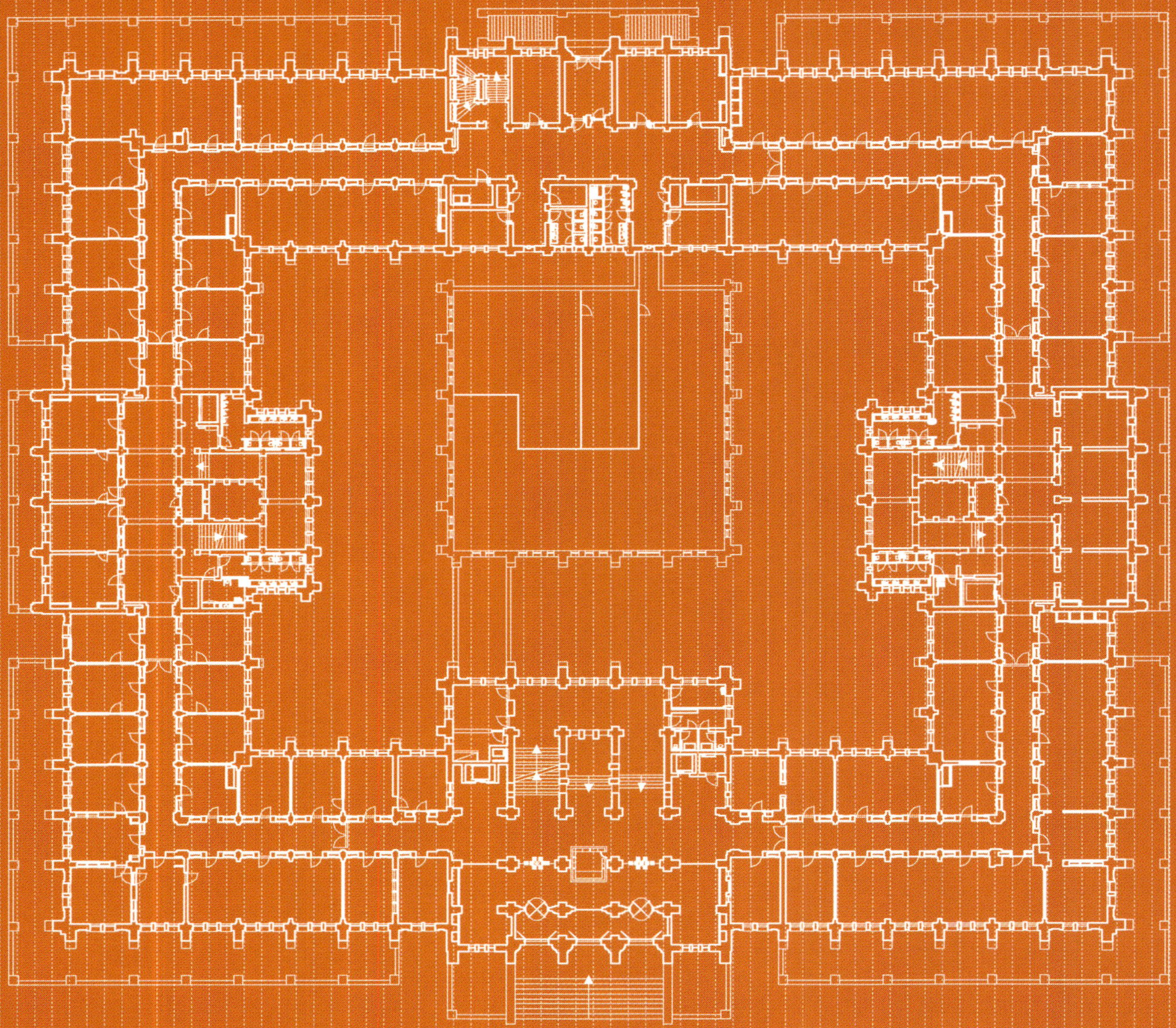

DE INKTPOT UTRECHT, 1:750
1 UNIT = 1.65 METER

De Inktpot ('The Inkwell')
Client: Railinfrabeheer, Verkeersleiding and Railned (three branches
of Dutch Railways) Location: Moreelse park 1, Utrecht
Restoration architect: Van Stigt Architects
Interior architect: Merkx+Girod Architects
Project team: Evelyne Merkx, Bert de Munnik, Trudy Tijs,
Hans Tomassen (Aswa Architects), Jan Willem Wijker
General contractor: Strukton
Graphics (signage): Merkx+Girod Architects, Bureau Mijksenaar
Graphics (pantries, entrance area, lettering, and numbering):
Merkx+Girod Architects, René Knip
Furniture: Merkx+Girod Architects, Keijsers Interior Projects
Project duration: 2.5 years

Completion: October 2002
Photography: Roos Aldershoff

PLANCIUS

Formerly the home of Jewish choral society *Oefening Baart Kunst* ('Practice Makes Perfect'), the 19th-century building in question currently accommodates the Resistance Museum and café-restaurant Plancius.

The project involved a distinctive, elongated space with a high ceiling, robust supporting beams and a façade that was to be preserved in its original state. The clients – the same hospitality-industry duo that established Spanjer & van Twist, an earlier project of ours – clearly stated their objective: a café-restaurant with a nice atmosphere for an affordable price.

An aubergine leatherette banquette with a high rear wall for comfort and acoustics, cyclamen bolsters as accents, an open area where tabletops feature bold circles, industrial light boxes that underscore the rhythm of the steel beams, a bright yellow alcove in a black MDF wall for water bottles, and a lined blackboard for specials and the menu of the day. *Voilà!* Plancius.

The image is sober, urban and natural, but that 'natural look' is pure pretence. To heighten the sense of space, our top priority, we assembled a complete architectural box, inserted it into the building and left the existing ceiling untouched. The wall that serves as a backrest for the high banquette is a freestanding element that screens the entrance to the toilets and the dishwashing kitchen.

The textual image covering one wall is a design by Annelies Frölke.

Plancius
Clients: Hans van Twist, Dick Spanjer
Location: Plantage Kerklaan 61, Amsterdam
Interior architect: Merkx+Girod Architects
Project team: Patrick Bento, Josje Kuiper, Evelyne Merkx,
Jan Willem Wijker
General contractor: IJskes
Graphics: Annelies Frölke
Floor area: 200m²
Project duration: 1 year
Completion: 2001
Photography: Roos Aldershoff

THE GLORY OF THE GOLDEN AGE, JUBILEE EXHIBITION AT THE RIJKSMUSEUM IN AMSTERDAM

For *The Glory of the Golden Age*, an exhibition that celebrated the 200th anniversary of the Rijksmuseum in Amsterdam, we designed suspended partitions and selected their colours from the backgrounds of Renaissance paintings by Bellini and Titian. Indeed, it was a sudden change in style – this Carpaccio red, Vecellio blue and Bellini green – from traditional liver-coloured hues. Owing to the vibrancy and exceptional depth of the pigments, some of which originated in the 18th century, we applied the paint in layers and used a finishing coat of wax.

To reinforce the unifying effect of the partitions – the museum's exhibition spaces vary in form and dimension – we opted to make all steel-framed partitions the same size and to paint all rear walls a warm shade of grey. One room, being too low, managed to evade this scenario. Completely wrapped in golden-yellow – ceiling, walls and floor – it became a little jewellery box, so to speak.

Our proposal for *The Night Watch* – a deep, vibrant green to replace the cool grey that had served as a backdrop for years – met with a wall of protest that included the board of directors. A view of the computer simulation, however, convinced the lot. Strangely enough, we later discovered that Cuypers, the architect of the Rijksmuseum, had chosen dark green for this hall in his original plan.

We envisioned ceramic objects on floating pedestals, but even a guarantee of stable construction wasn't enough for the decision-makers, who could not bear the thought of their vulnerable, rare and costly exhibits taking a tumble. So we gave the platforms a supporting base. Graphic design – bold numbers indicating the various halls, and mottoes high on the walls – was the work of Irma Boom*.

°Dutch graphic designer whose furore-causing
activities include work for Vitra, AKZO,
the De Appel Foundation (Amsterdam), Stroom
(a visual-arts centre in The Hague), and KPN.

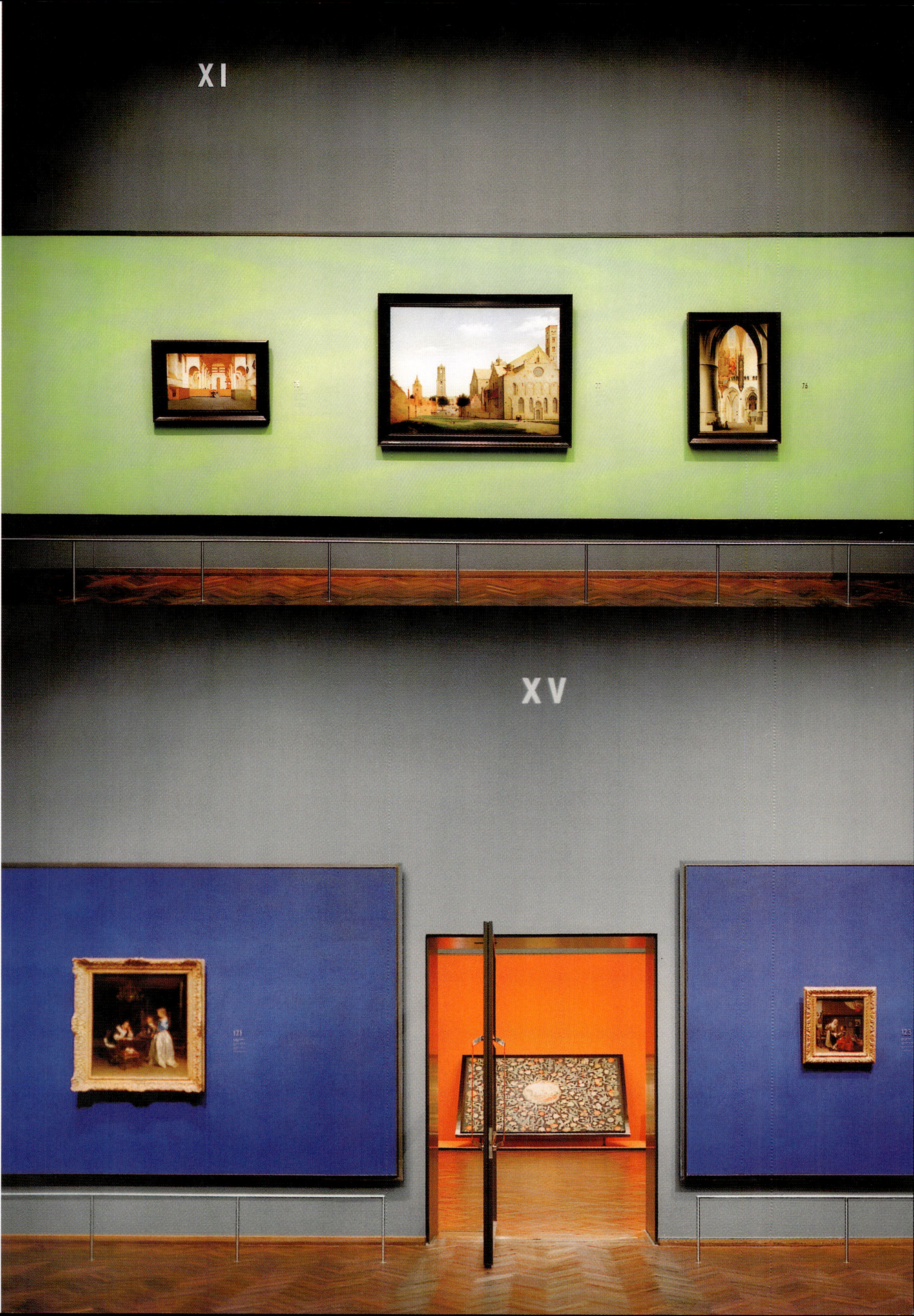
XI
XV

The Glory of the Golden Age
Client: Rijksmuseum
Location: Stadhouderkskade 42, Amsterdam
Interior architect: Merkx+Girod Architects
Project team: Patrice Girod, Marleen Inia, Josje Kuiper,
Evelyne Merkx, Det van Oers
Graphics: Irma Boom
Project duration: 7 months
Exhibition dates: April 15 - September 17, 2000
Photography: Roos Aldershoff

HEMA NIEUWENDIJK, AMSTERDAM

HEMA

One day in late 1995 we got a phone call. Would we make an analysis of HEMA department stores in the country's larger cities? Turnover in the big cities was stagnating. Sure, we'd love to. 'Doing' the HEMA had always been on our wish list HEMA is a fantastic department store. Founded in 1926 as *Hollandse Eenheidsprijzen Maatschappij Amsterdam* ('Dutch Uniform-Price Association Amsterdam'), it remains a no-nonsense organisation that offers a wide range of inexpensive HEMA-brand products. Household items, clothing and food. Good sellers are underwear, washing powder, wine and smoked sausage. The store's buyers are veritable sleuths with good taste and a nose for quality. All classes of society patronise the store; no one thinks she's too good for candles from the HEMA. Another strong point is the 'no good, money back' policy, which is followed without hesitation.

All right. An analysis. We started our tour of the country with a camera adjusted to a height of 1.70 metres (Evelyne's eye level) and focused on matters such as entrance, display window and application of the HEMA logo. In short, we took a good look at the welcome mat. What we found both inside and out was as bad as it gets, a real mess.
All kinds of lamps dangled from cheap and often damaged modular ceilings. Floors were dirty. Dust on the upper shelves had been ignored. Cash desks – the ones that could be found – displayed no clear indication of where the queue started, a situation that caused irritation and even arguments during busier shopping hours. Customers tripped over displays and searched in vain for information on what and where. As far as we could see, each HEMA operated according to its own system, but nowhere was a genuine welcome part of the approach.

In February 1996 we presented our findings, along with a strategy that featured proposals for improvement. The board of directors promised to consider the matter in due time. Less than a month later, however, we got another call. The HEMA had decided, at the last minute, to participate in the development of a new subterranean shopping centre in Rotterdam, the Beurstraverse, now more popularly known by the Dutch equivalent of 'Bargain Basement'. Could we apply our recently presented findings to the new outlet, which had to be completed in five months? One heck of a job, of course, but also a golden opportunity.

HEMA NIEUWENDIJK, AMSTERDAM, 1:400
1 UNIT = 1 M

HEMA NIEUWENDIJK

Our next chance to apply the concept was in the former home of an old general store renowned in the Netherlands – De Winkel van Sinkel – a building on Nieuwendijk, in the heart of Amsterdam. Although a highly attractive structure in essence, the building was completely dilapidated. We were determined to free the beautiful glass roof, invisible from the ground floor because of intervening floors, a task that would allow natural light to enter the store. The question was how?
We finally decided to conceal all mechanical systems and to create a succession of voids or, in other words, one towering volume of empty space. Surrounding the void on the first floor are retail facilities and a restaurant. The void above hides the mechanical systems. And the third-floor void, which lies directly below the glass roof, is encircled by offices.
Wherever you stand you can see the HEMA-blue rear wall, complete with clock and logo, as well as the glass roof, which opens the entire space to a flood of natural light. Thanks to a light shaft on the top floor, which draws light from the side into the offices and, from there, into the shopping areas, the glass roof seems to be elevated in the air. A light, airy, open design without an objectionable element in sight.
To get the desired result, we spent an incredible amount of time shifting the parts of our model from one spot to another. Finally we had a space that resembled the layered structure of a music score, particularly because the extended void, as seen from below, tapers slightly as it ascends to clear the way for the upward glance and the light spilling down.

HEMA Nieuwendijk
Client: HEMA Amsterdam bv
Location: Nieuwendijk 174-176, Amsterdam
Architect and interior architect: Merkx+Girod Architects
Project team: Joost Arts, Matthijs van Cruijsen, Mark van der Geest,
Patrice Girod, Evelyne Merkx, Leendert Spreij (Aswa Architects),
Ton Wandel (Aswa Architects)
General contractor: Midreth Construction Company
Graphics: Merkx+Girod Architects, René Knip, Agata Zwierzyńska
Furniture: Merkx+Girod Architects, Wageningen Meubel & Interieurbouw
Project duration: 2 years
Completion: 1998
Photography: Roos Aldershoff (snack counter), Alexander van Berge

HEMA ROTTERDAM (DUTCH PILOT STORE)

Essential points of the concept are clarity and surveyability. See what you get, beginning with the shop windows. No cute little displays but a bold presentation of special offers in bulk. From shampoo to deck chairs. We filled in the retail floor with low display elements that give customers a good view of the space, including high wall displays with large photographic panels illustrating the products sold in various sections of the store. These visuals function like pictograms: easy to see, easy to understand. As do the clustered cash desks, whose bright-red rear walls indicate their location.

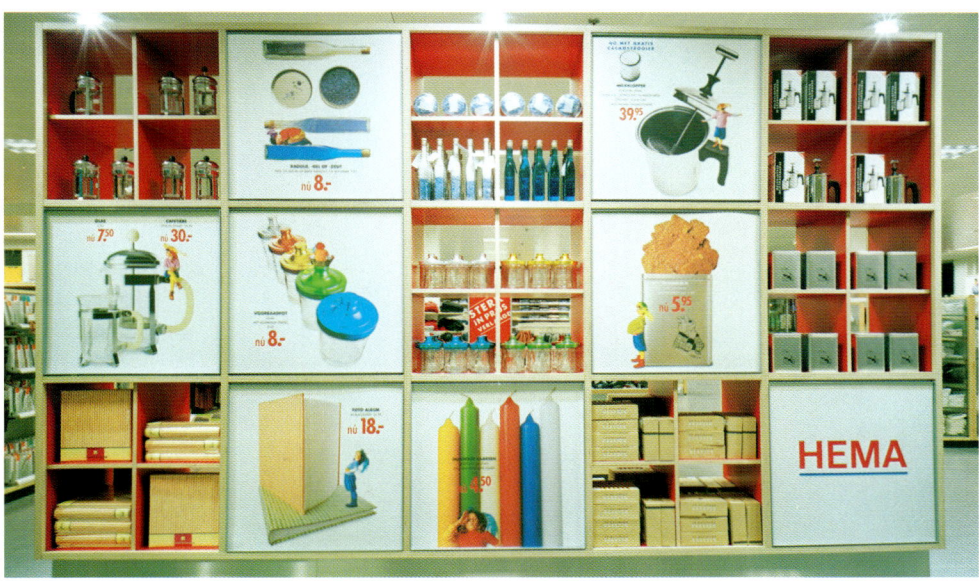

Distinction and simplicity characterise the materials used – light wood, aluminium and flooring tile – as well as the bright colours and the white backgrounds of the product photos. Decorative elements are scarce. An exception to the rule is the area next to the escalators, where we went all out. Having asked illustrator Agatha Zwierzyńska to sketch typical HEMA products, we displayed huge enlargements of her drawings on coloured panels.

HEMA Rotterdam
Client: HEMA Amsterdam bv
Location: Beursplein 2, Rotterdam
Interior architect: Merkx+Girod Architects
Project team: Matthijs van Cruijsen, Mark van der Geest,
Patrice Girod, Evelyne Merkx
Furniture: Merkx+Girod Architects, Benschop
Graphics: Merkx+Girod Architects, René Knip
Project duration: 5 months
Completion: 1996
Photography: Pieter Vlamings

We wanted the 'see what you get' approach which is reflected in HEMA's advertising as well. The idea required a correlation between the existing HEMA brochures dropped in people's mailboxes and the panels reserved for special offers, which hang above high display elements in the store.

We were thrilled to be able to implement the concept virtually without compromise. There was simply no time for squabbles. Even the sandwich counter that we wanted to add to the HEMA formula – an element based on London's Pret A Mangers and one that the board had initially vetoed – was ultimately realised. Graphics for the food department are the work of René Knip.

Management decided to use our concept as a starting point for an all-out reorganisation of HEMA stores in major Dutch cities. But first we made a detour to Antwerp. HEMA wanted to open a chain of outlets in Belgium, and we were asked to develop a concept for the pilot store.

HEMA ANTWERP (BELGIAN PILOT STORE)

The building that accommodates the first Belgian HEMA is exceedingly elongated. We emphasised the form by installing a 'street of light' the entire length of the premises. This element, along with a rear door, gives the store the character of a shopping gallery. Although the concept provides guidelines, it is not a straitjacket. Each outlet is able to respond to the particular circumstances marking its location. The experiment in Antwerp achieved its purpose. Belgium currently boasts 24 HEMA outlets. (The Netherlands has 255.)

DESIGN MANUAL FOR RENOVATIONS IN THE NETHERLANDS

After realising HEMA outlets in Rotterdam, Antwerp and Amsterdam Nieuwendijk, we were commissioned to develop a design manual for renovations throughout the Netherlands. We left nothing to chance. Ceilings, furniture, lighting, tiles – the tiniest detail can be found in the manual.

HEMA plans to continue the process using in-house services. But will they preserve the purity of the concept? Unfortunately, we already have indications to the contrary.

HEMA Antwerp
Client: HEMA Amsterdam bv
Location: Meir 35, Antwerp, Belgium
Interior architect: Merkx+Girod Architects
Project team: Matthijs van Cruijsen, Mark van cer Geest,
Patrice Girod, Evelyne Merkx, Ton Wandel (Aswa Architects)
Graphics: Merkx+Girod Architects, René Knip
Furniture: Merkx+Girod Architects, Wageningen Meubel & Interieurbouw
Project duration: 2 years
Completion: 1997
Photography: Pieter Vlamings

STUDIO EDELKOORT

My first project for Lidewij Edelkoort* was the conversion of a former factory
for artificial limbs (a company in Paris that had stopped 'running' profitably)
into a studio.
A partition wall of steel and curved glass, both tinted and clear – custom-made
in the Netherlands and transported to France – embraces a new stairway designed
to eliminate the complicated slalom between spaces. A floor reminiscent of
Carl André's steel works of art is simply blocks of black and brown linoleum.
The stairway remains unrealised; the client came up with a different idea. The
recess now holds a piece of sculpture.

*Trend-watcher and founder of Trend Union,
Studio Edelkoort, United Publishers and
Heartwear. Chairwoman of the Design Academy in
Eindhoven.

100

Studio Edelkoort
Client: Lidewij Edelkoort
Location: 30, Boulevard Saint Jacques, Paris, France
Interior architect: Studio Merkx
Project team: Evelyne Merkx, Patrice Girod
Smith: Coevert
Project duration: 1 year
Completion: 1987
Photography: Roos Aldershoff

SPANJER & VAN TWIST RESTAURANT

Informal eatery in the heart of the Jordaan, an old working-class neighbourhood in Amsterdam that has evolved into a popular residential and entertainment area. The trick was to maintain the flow of daylight that enters the space through extremely high windows in the kitchen, while blocking the view of the kitchen itself. The solution was a partition wall of steel and coloured glass. Collaborating with us on this project was Branko Vlamings.

Spanjer & van Twist Restaurant
Clients: Dick Spanjer, Hans van Twist
Location: Leliegracht 60h, Amsterdam
Interior architect: Studio Merkx
Project team: Josje Kuiper, Evelyne Merkx, Branko Vlamings,
Jan Willem Wijker
Steel partition wall: Merkx+Girod Architects
Smith: Koos van Wengerden
Floor area: 80m²
Project duration: 1 year
Completion: 1994
Photography: Pieter Vlamings

ATHENAEUM BOOKSHOP

The renovation of the Athenaeum bookshop on the Spui, a project that Wiek Röling and I did for clients Johan Polak and Rob van Gennep, provided a welcome relief during the long period that preceded the approval of the canalside flats – waiting for that decision was an energy-draining experience. I wanted to design a bookshop that *I'd* like to visit. Not the kind of layout that you can oversee in a single glance, but a space that invites you to wander around, with cosy corners for reading. I even designed a special stool for the purpose. I'm delighted, of course, that the retail interior remains unchanged after 35 years of use. Only the stairway to the upper level has been closed off to prevent theft. H'm.

103

Athenaeum Bookshop
Clients: Johan Polak, Rob van Gennep
Location: Spui 14-16, Amsterdam
Architects and project team: Patrice Girod, Wiek Röling
Completion: 1967
Photography: Koen Wessing

CANALSIDE FLATS

This place on the canal was my first – *our* first – project. Abel Cahen and I were still students at Delft, and this job actually prompted us to set up our own company. The commission was for a new canalside property with four flats plus business accommodations, and we worked on it for ages. Simply exhausting. It was the first modernist post-war building within Amsterdam's ring of canals, and the agency that regulates the appearance of buildings took a very dim view of our plans. They didn't like the concrete that we wanted to use – they didn't like anything. Initially, we reacted to the criticism by trying to improve the design one more time, but at a certain moment it's done, finished, complete.

After waiting five endless years for the building to be erected, we felt as though we'd won the marathon. Fortunately, the client supported us throughout – we submitted our plan ten times – and when the design was finally realised, we got terrific reviews in the press, both at home and abroad. It took us quite a while to recover from that ordeal.

Canalside Flats
Client: Tentler & Co
Location: Singel 428, Amsterdam
Architect: Cahen & Girod
Project team: Abel Cahen, Patrice Girod, Jan Koning
General contractor: Gruppen
Project duration: 7 years
Completion: 1971
Photography: Roos Aldershoff

ARBONED, UTRECHT

ARBONED

ArboNed, a rapidly expanding employment service that deals with healthcare and includes company doctors, leases a standard, ten-a-penny office space. Fine. But the organisation's management understands that an office like this demands a distinctive, well-appointed interior.

To provide the company's many visitors with a cheerful environment, we used images that revolve around 'being sick' as opposed to 'getting better'. Prevention versus ergonomics. We went on to develop visual materials in collaboration with Bureau Mijksenaar*, which also designed a signage system for the premises.

The 18 consultation rooms that we scattered throughout the space like little boxes are adorned, on the entrance side, with blow-ups of pill strips, capsules, safety gear and the famed kinetic studies of photographer Eadweard Muybridge. We also used enlarged drawings by industrial designer Dreyfuss, widely considered to be the father of ergonomics. A scarlet rug in the reception hall features human figures from Ernst Neufert's manual for architects, which his son gave us permission to use. More of these drawings, in which all sorts of human activities are set down in sizes and numbers, can be found in the company restaurant. To liven up the endless hallways, we also added blow-ups to the walls of cabinets that form a boundary between corridor and consultation room.

A visual theme, even one that's particularly striking, isn't enough, however. Our next task was to design special partition walls of aluminium and glass, which make a seamless connection to the silver-grey ceiling system, a metal surface with built-in lighting. The cream-coloured stone floor complements a distinguished reception counter and reading table. Once across the threshold, the visitor has nothing to remind him of the uniformity that characterises a standard office shell.

*A company specialising in visual communications and well-known
for, among other things, postage-stamp design, pictograms
and signage for Schiphol Airport.

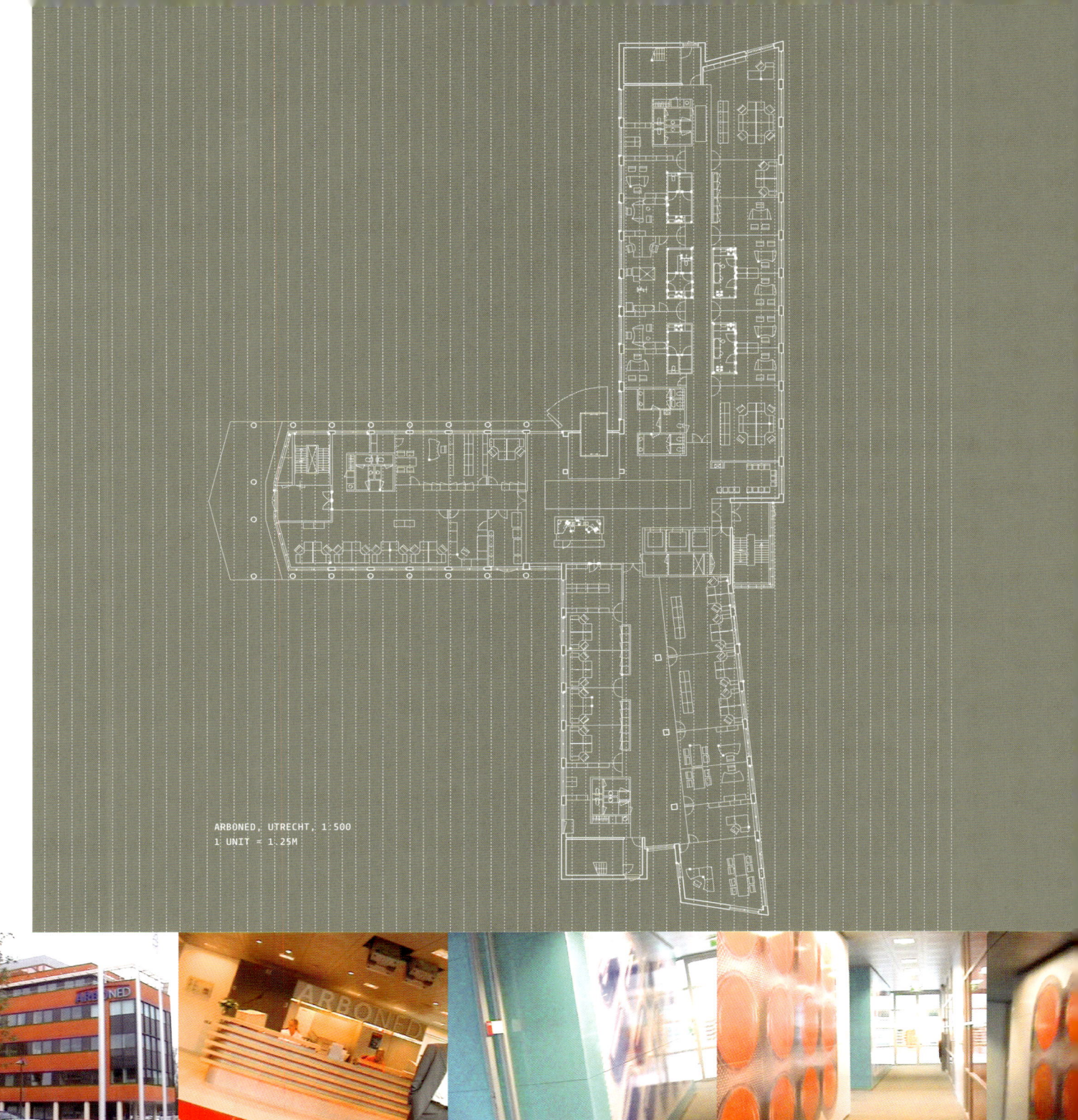

ARBONED, UTRECHT, 1:500
1 UNIT = 1.25M

bar
open

(en waarmee we ons hier even niet mee zullen bezighouden

en fruitbestek; de aanduidingen spreken voor zichzelf. Ten slotte is

kreeft, grote en kleine slakken. Het dekken va

De vorken liggen links van het bord, het desert- en fruitbestek

erscheiden we groot bestek, klein bestek,

og bijzonder   bestek voor het eten

bestek is, anders dan men wel denkt, doode

ven, de messen "snijkant

rich

de volgorde waarin het

022

Fig 12.6 Posities ~~~ de arm en hand bij rekoefeningen voor~~ de elleboog: A de hand ligt in het verleng~~ van de onderarm met de handrug naar ~~~; B de handrug is naar boven wordt ~~~rekt; C de hand ligt in het verlengde va~~ onderarm met de

ArboNed
Client: ArboNed
Location: Zwarte Woud 10, Utrecht
Interior architect: Merkx+Girod Architects
Project team: Patrick Bento, Mark van der Geest, Patrice Girod,
Josje Kuiper, Evelyne Merkx, Ton Wandel (Aswa Architects)
Signage: Bureau Mijksenaar
Graphics: Merkx+Girod Architects, Bureau Mijksenaar
Carpet design (entrance): Merkx+Girod Architects, Joost Grootens
Floor area: 7000m²
Project duration: 2 years
Completion: 2000
Photography: Roos Aldershoff

Spine
Designer: Evelyne Merkx
Manufacturer: Bulo
Completion: 1998
Material: walnut wood
Dimensions: w 3090 × d 900 × h 750mm
Production: part of the Carte Blanche series

SPINE

In addition to its usual line of products, Bulo – a Belgian manufacturer of office furniture – also markets the Carte Blanche collection, which consists of tables created by different designers, not all of whom specialise in furniture or interior design. My table is just one of a very impressive series. Others who were given 'carte blanche' by Bulo include Maarten van Severen, Bob van Reeth, Ann Demeulemeester and Jean Nouvel.

I call my design Spine, because the piece has a distinct backbone. Connections at the junction of tabletop and base are clearly visible. Leaving them visible allowed me to accentuate the form of the 3-metre-long-plus table, which has two legs at either end and a pair of legs on both sides. Both tabletop (42cm thick) and legs are made of walnut wood with a rich surface grain.

Worth mentioning is that Bulo opted for a showroom in a former peanut-roasting factory in Amsterdam that we had already renovated. Luc Vincent designed the interior for Bulo.

Bulo Showroom
Client: Bulo Belgium (Head office)
Location: Westerstraat 252-254, Amsterdam
Interior architect: Luc Vincent
Project team: Tjade Binnerts, Patrice Girod, Evelyne Merkx
Renovation: Merkx+Girod Architects
Completion: 2000
Photography: Roos Aldershoff

TRIMP & VAN TARTWIJK, IJSSELSTEIN

TRIMP & VAN TARTWIJK

Historic premises à la *Hansel and Gretel* – hardly a match for the status of the property developer moving into the place. What's more, the relatively small space was completely silted up, so to speak. Our slogan was 'Light, air and long live the present!' – a concept that the client immediately embraced as his own. An important intervention was the construction of a translucent waiting room that provides an online hook-up for laptops. Although some functions do require privacy, we attempted to achieve that goal without creating a claustrophobic composition of closed cubicles. We relied on transparent partitions and installed windows in the thick walls separating certain areas. The result is an office that forms a spatial entity.

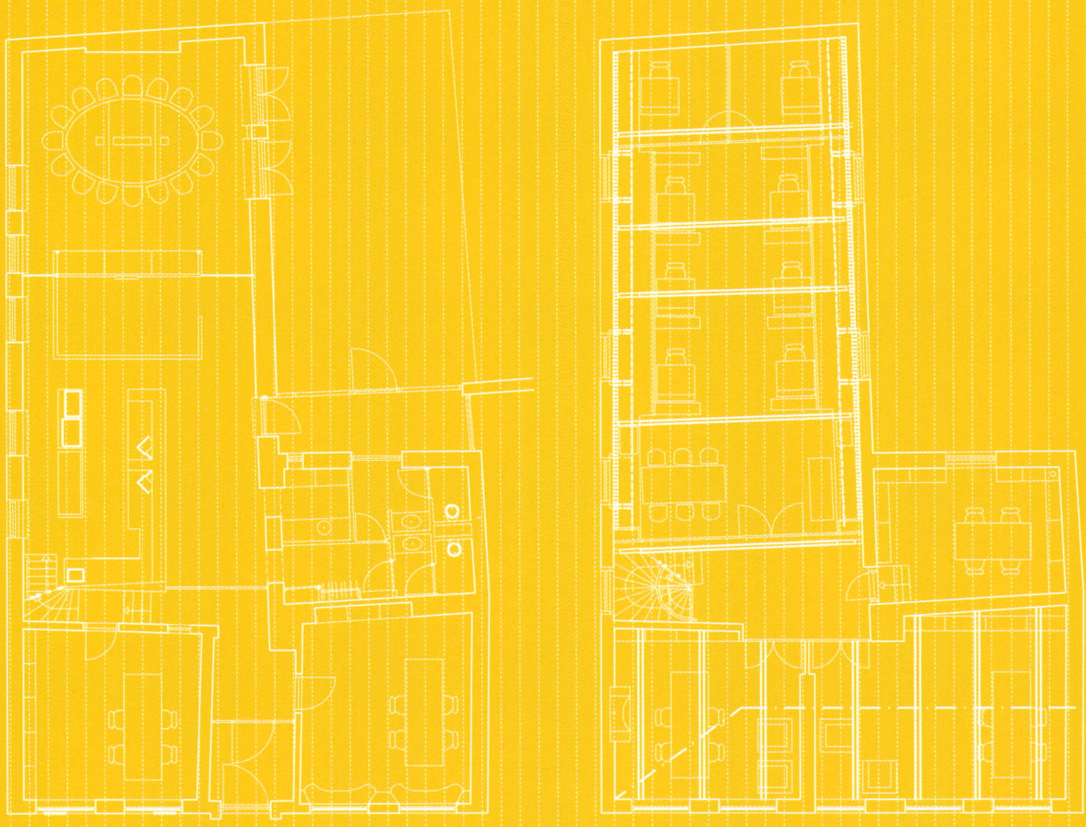

TRIMP & VAN TARTWIJK, IJSSELSTEIN
GROUND AND FIRST FLOOR 1:200
2 UNITS = 1 METER

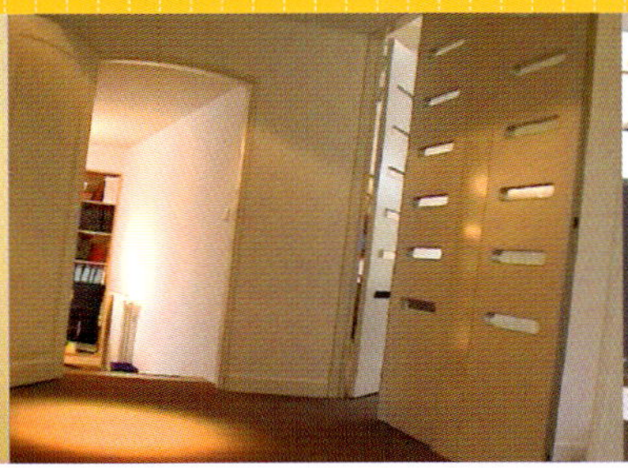
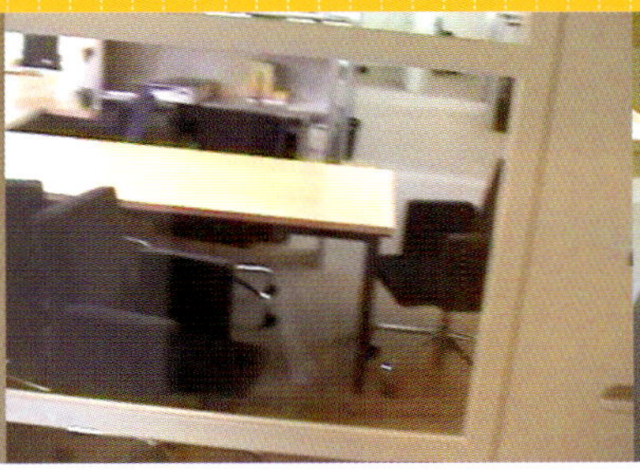
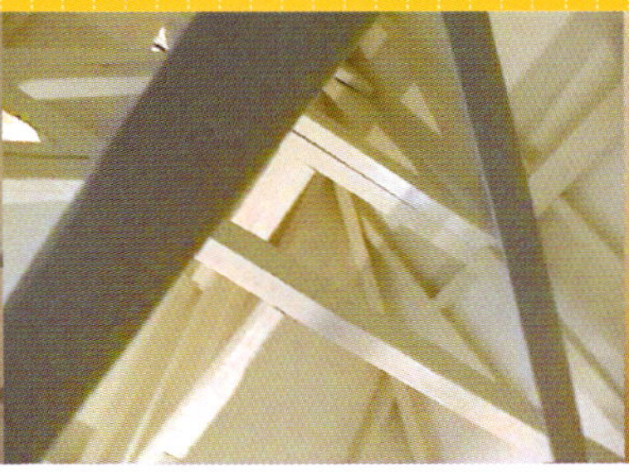
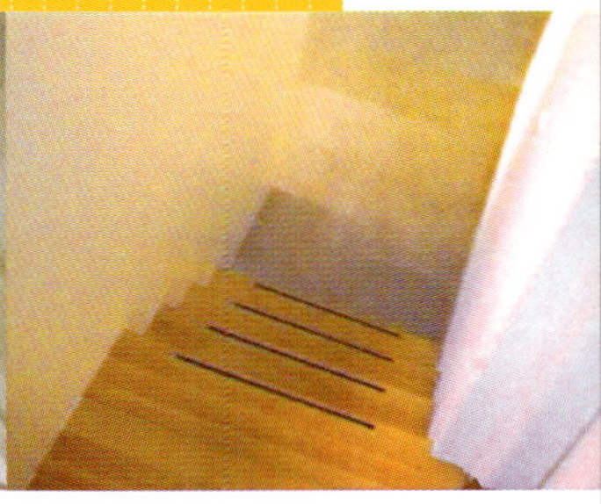

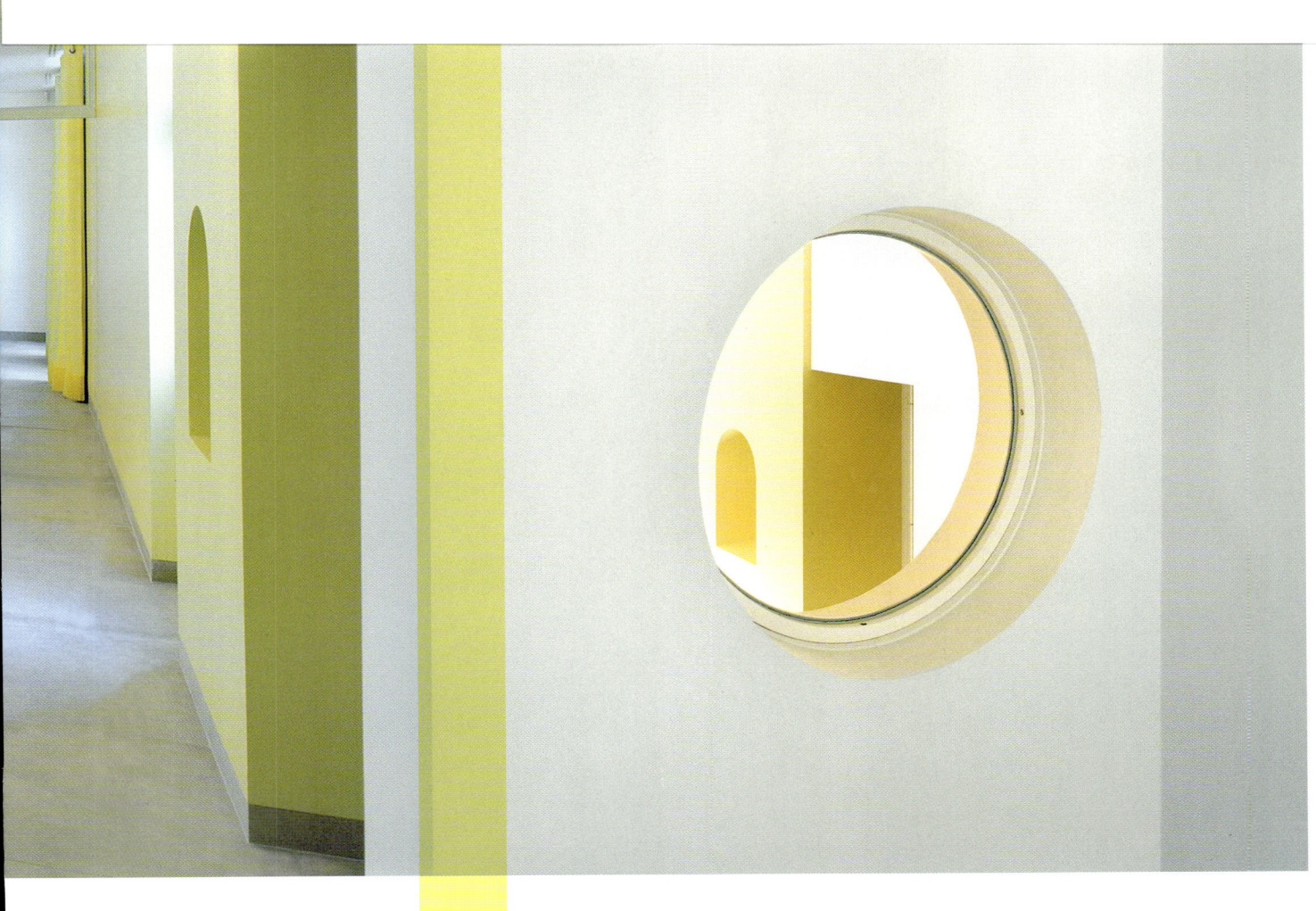

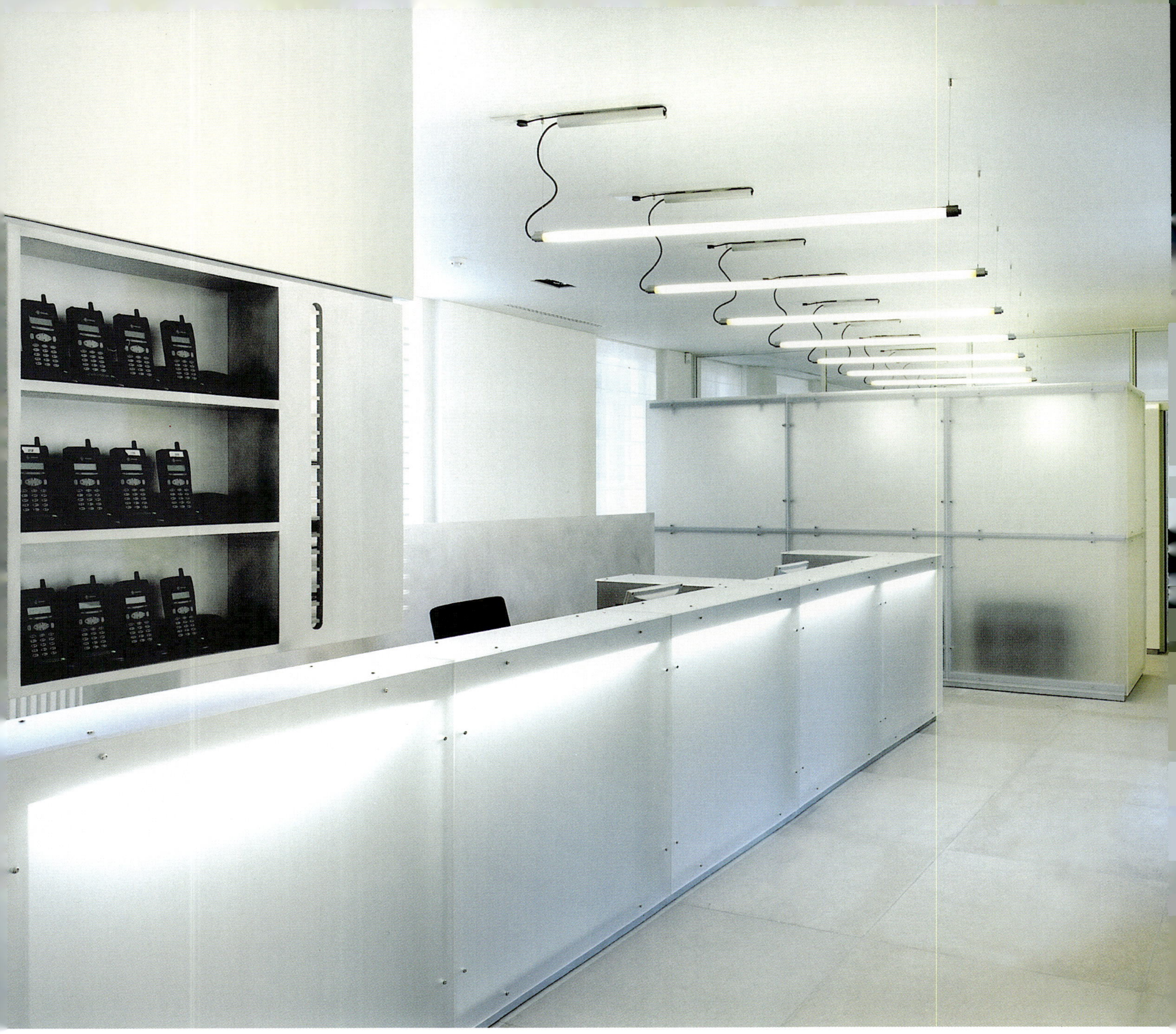

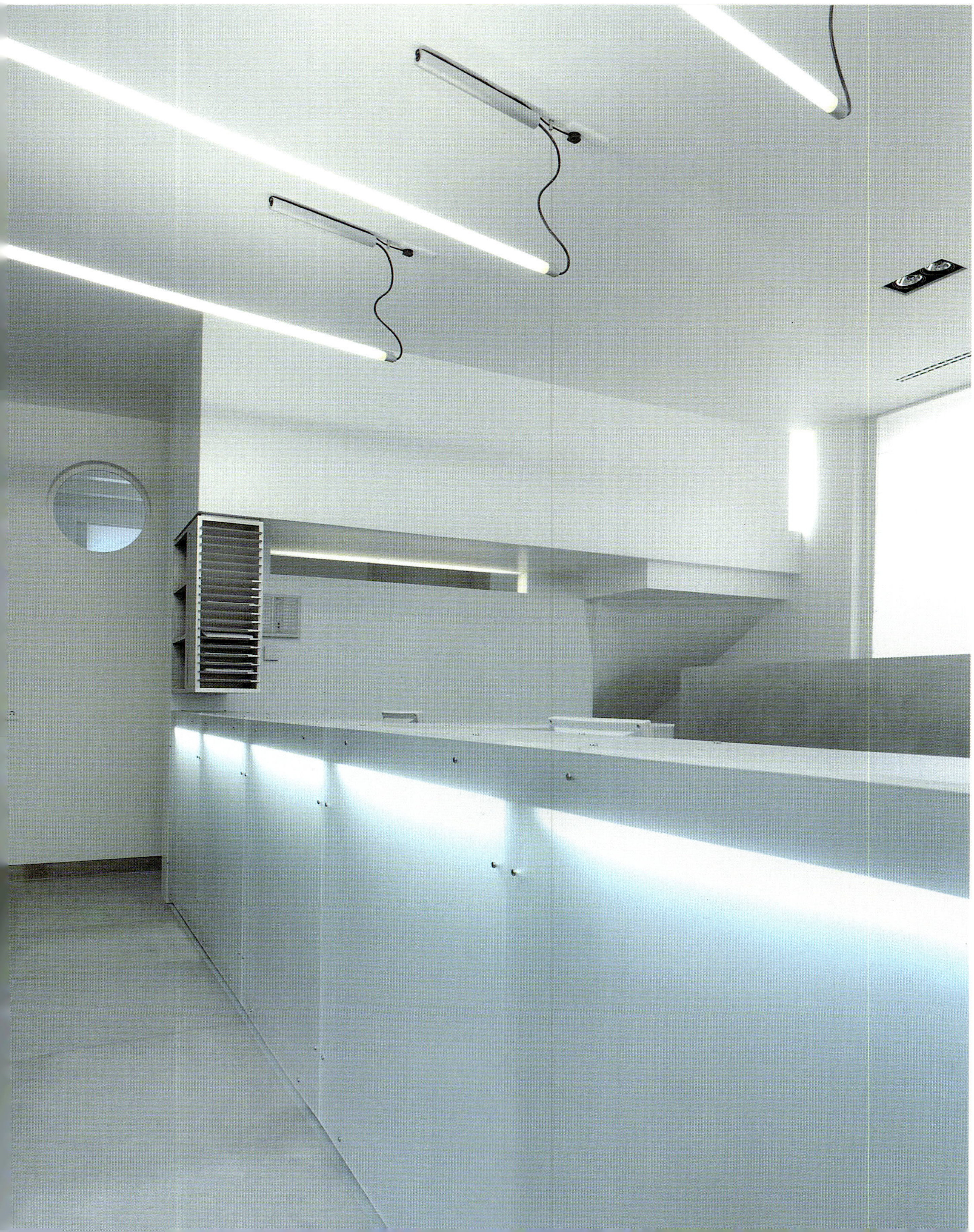

Trimp & Van Tartwijk
Client: Trimp & van Tartwijk
Location: Kronenburgplantsoen 10, IJsselstein
Interior architect: Merkx+Girod Architects
Project team: Patrice Girod, Marleen Inia, Josje Kuiper,
Evelyne Merkx, Jan Willem Wijker
Floor area: 400m²
Project duration: 1.5 years
Completion: 2001
Photography: Roos Aldershoff

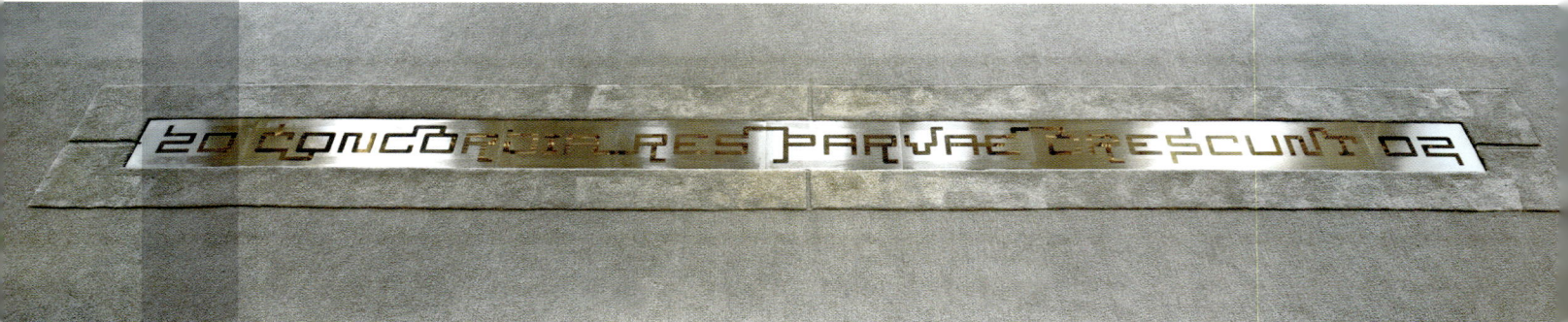

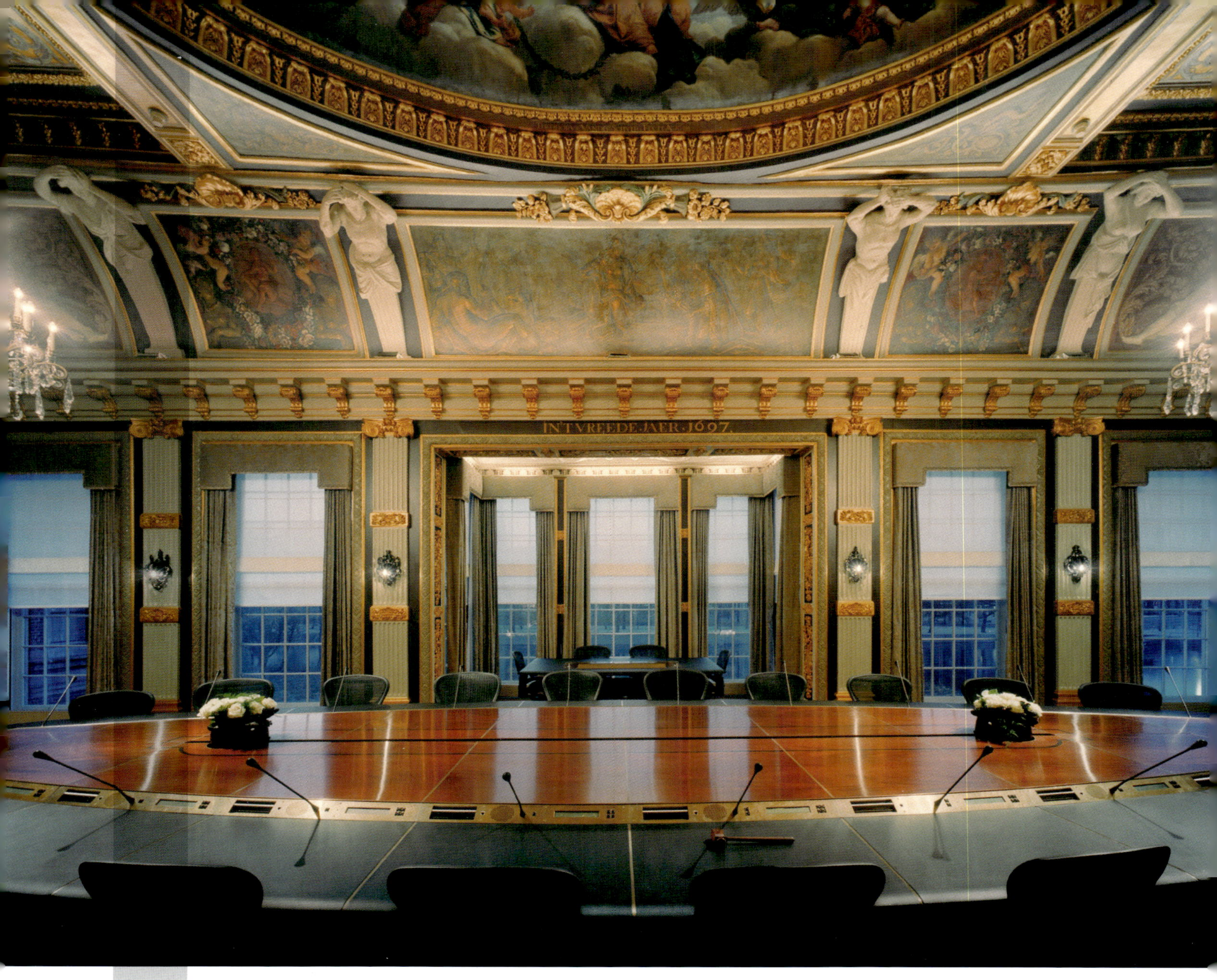
IN'T VREEDE JAER 1697

20 CONCORDIA RES PARVAE CRESCUNT 02

TRÊVES HALL

Anything but an ordinary venue, Trêves Hall is the permanent assembly hall of the Dutch Council of Ministers. In the past, however, it was not a place that offered a great deal of comfort. The table was too low, its legs were awkwardly positioned, and the chairs were too heavy. Furthermore, cabinet ministers had a hard time hearing what was being said and often had to crane their necks around table lamps to see one another. Nor did they appreciate the purple skirt around the table, a device used to keep cables out of sight. It bore an eerie resemblance to a shroud.

Thanks to our (successful) presentation of a design for the extension and renovation of the Council of State, the Government Building Agency recommended Merkx+Girod for the renovation of the Trêves Hall.

The refurbishment of this space, which Daniel Marot had completely decorated with paintings in 1697, was not an easy job. An important precondition was to create a design that would relate to its neoclassical surroundings. And a hall sometimes used for official receptions had to be able to be cleared quickly – preferably in the blink of an eye. The programme of technical requirements represented yet another predicament.

We made an extensive study of various table forms and the sight lines they provide, finally opting for an oval table, consisting of 18 components, whose mahogany top is inlaid with black-leather desk pads. We integrated the mechanical systems (microphone, speaker, mute button for private conversation, LCD monitor and so forth) into a raised, bronze-plated element. Twelve video screens can be clicked into the middle of the tabletop.

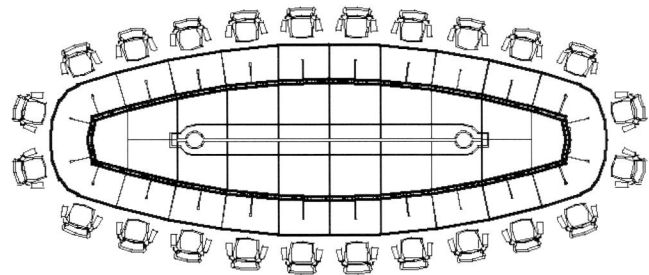

Trêves Hall
Client: Government Building Agency
Location: Binnenhof, The Hague
Interior architect: Merkx+Girod Architects
Project team: Patrice Girod, Josje Kuiper, Evelyne Merkx, Det van Oers
Carpet design: Merkx+Girod Architects, M3
Carpet manufacturer: Treutlein Carpets
Graphics: Merkx+Girod Architects, René Knip
Vases and wall lighting: Merkx+Girod Architects, Bernard Heesen
Furniture: Merkx+Girod Architects, Wageningen Meubel & Interieurbouw,
Bronnenberg Staalbouw, Koos van Wengerden
Chandelier: Schonbek
Lighting: Erco

Bronzing: Heijchroom
Curtains: Multi Decorations
Audio: Jacot Technology
Floor area: 150m²
Project duration: 1.5 years
Completion: 2002
Photography: Teo Krijgsman

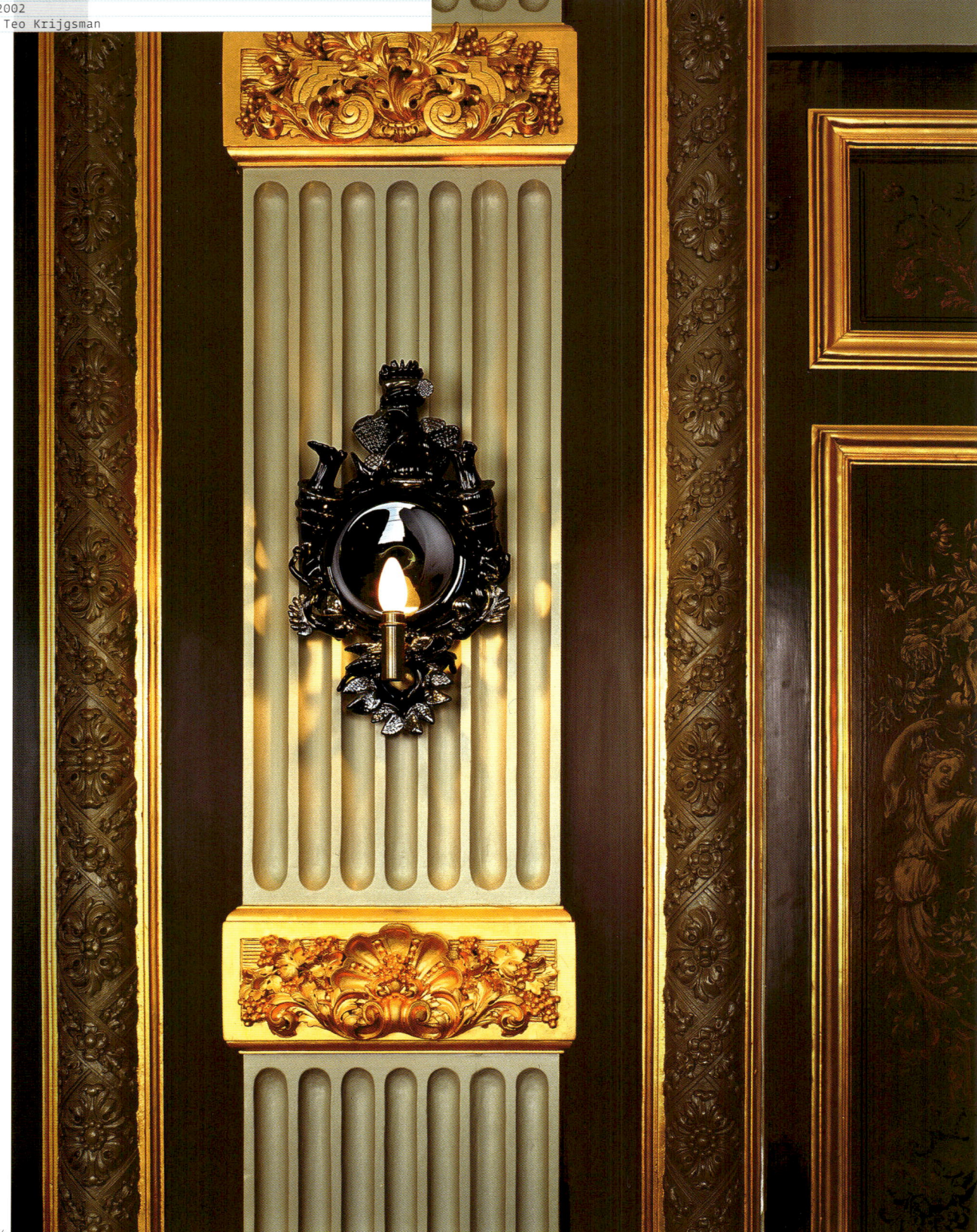

We asked artist Bernard Heesen, who works in glass, to design vases for the obligatory flower arrangements. His creations are recessed into the tabletop. Heesen also designed new wall lamps of black glass. Just two examples of the many custom-made details that characterise this project. Having solved the problem of the table, we moved on to another complicated issue: illumination. The ministers need light to see one another clearly, to view video presentations and to read written material without eyestrain. Not to mention that the window with a view of the pond outside creates a bright backlight at times. We covered the windows with translucent Venetian curtains made of batiste, and designed a sophisticated lighting system featuring two Louis XIV-style crystal chandeliers that combine atmospheric lighting with dimmable halogen spots aimed at the individual desk pads. Manufactured in the United States, the chandeliers boast suspended ornaments of Bohemian crystal. What we found so interesting about this project was the number of problems that demanded *real* solutions. And although the clients were somewhat reserved at the outset, their enthusiasm grew by leaps and bounds as the work progressed. We asked the ministers to participate in all intervening stages of the project, regularly inviting them to view computer simulations and proposals for colour schemes. The idea worked. Take the example of our conviction that a good contemporary design does nothing to adversely affect a historical environment, but actually contributes to it – an opinion that was not accepted without question. After intensive consultation with everyone up to and including the Prime Minister, however, the current consensus is that Herman Miller's Aeron chair provides the best seat in the house.

BOS MEN SHOP 1997

Bos Men Shop is a de luxe establishment with striking features: a steel shop front with integrated name, sliding doors with horizontal panels and a suspended steel staircase whose steps continue into a massive block that accommodates the fitting rooms.

BOS MEN SHOP 2000

In 2000 we renovated the original Bos Men Shop, which is housed in a freestanding, imitation-Dutch, listed building adjacent to the marketplace – a splendid location, but a poorly organised interior. Making use of the existing steel construction, we developed a new interior around a void that nearly reaches the roof.

Bos Men Shop 1997
Client: Mr and Mrs Bos
Location: Lange Delft 37, Middelburg
Interior architect: Merkx+Girod Architects
Project team: Joop Bensdorp, Patrice Girod, Josje Kuiper, Evelyne Merkx, Jan Willem Wijker
Furniture and walls: Slabbekoorn Interieurbouw
Floor area: 225m²
Project duration: 9 months
Completion: 1997
Photography: Pieter Vlamings

Bos Men Shop 2000
Client: Mr and Mrs Bos
Location: Lange Delft 1, Middelburg
Interior architect: Merkx+Girod Architects
Project team: Stefan Bennebroek, Patrice Girod, Josje Kuiper,
Evelyne Merkx, Jan Willem Wijker
Lighting: Merkx+Girod Architects
Furniture and walls: Slabbekoorn Interieurbouw
Floor area: 220m²
Project duration: 9 months
Completion: 2000
Photography: Lajos Geenen

AMSTERDAM CONCERTGEBOUW

AMSTERDAM CONCERTGEBOUW ('CONCERT HALL')

If we are to believe the top names in music, the Main Hall of the Amsterdam Concertgebouw is an acoustic wonder of the world. Of course, the interior has been a bit shabby. In the Main Hall itself, wooden slats affixed to walls and ceiling were a desperate attempt to prevent cracks in the plaster from worsening. During the last renovation, in 1963, ceiling coffers were stripped of their plaster ornamentation (after a chunk of falling plaster nearly hit a musician) and reduced to unadorned squares with convex protrusions – the so-called 'flowerpots'. The ceiling was then painted egg-yolk yellow, a colour not in keeping with green side walls. Whisked away under a coat of brown paint, arched wall mouldings couldn't escape the inevitable nickname 'sandwiches'. According to the *NRC-Handelsblad* music editor, the audience was packed in a biscuit tin with the wrong lid.

In August 1995, as one of five architecture firms selected by Martijn Sanders, director of the Concertgebouw, we were asked to submit a renovation plan. Sanders knew we were capable of carrying out renovations under exceptional circumstances. That is exactly what was required in this case, as the programme of events scheduled to take place in the Concertgebouw was to remain unaffected by the renovation.

The project was not accompanied by a programme of requirements. We were asked to define the problems (not only in terms of aesthetics, but also from a logistic and technical point of view) before creating a master plan. Our master plan would apply to the entire interior: public areas as well as those behind the scenes. The core of the plan was and is (the operation will continue until 2006) the refurbishment of the Main Hall.

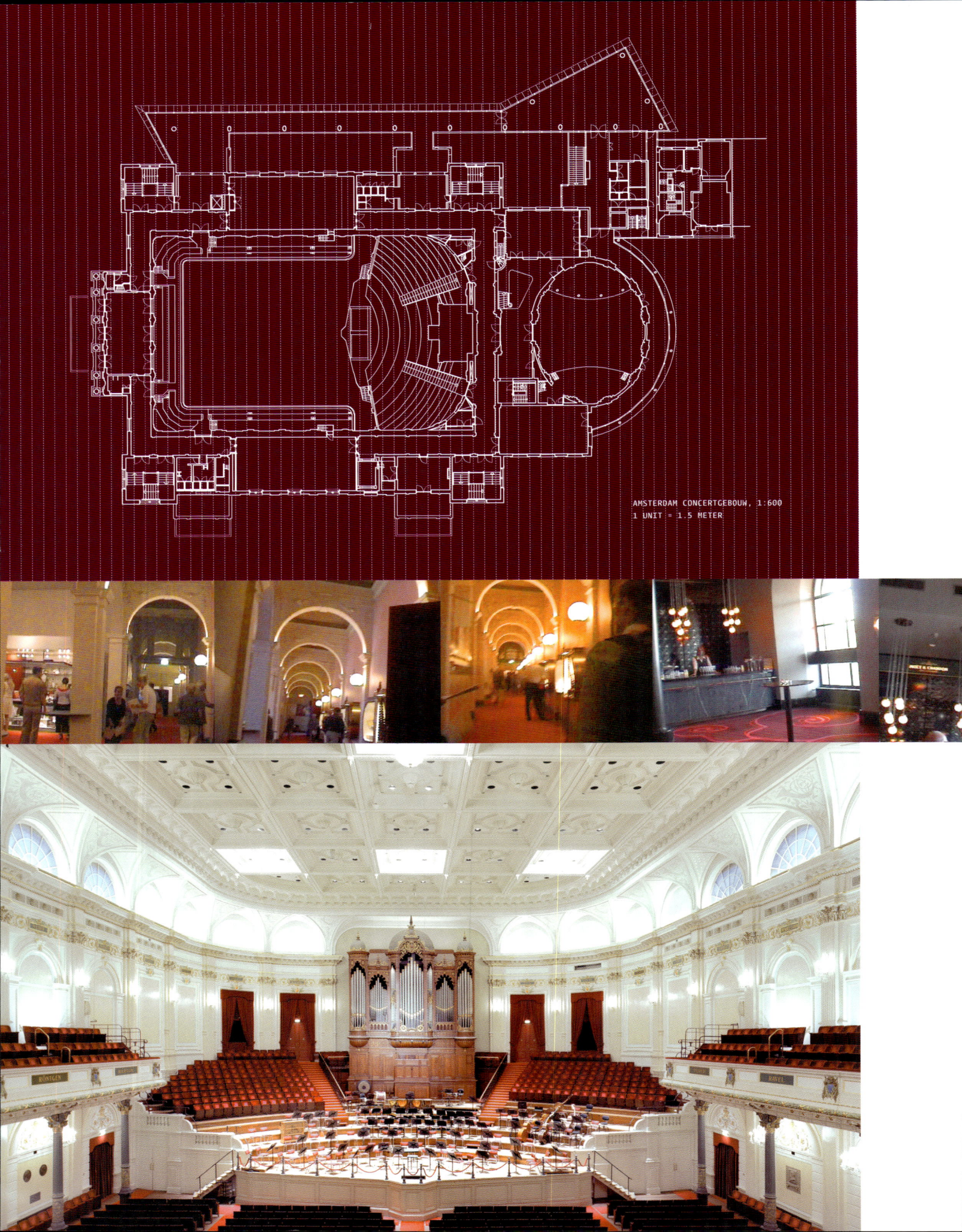

AMSTERDAM CONCERTGEBOUW, 1:600
1 UNIT = 1.5 METER

The Main Hall — what a hotchpotch! We didn't realise how bad it was until we'd taken photos of the interior by daylight, minus the presence of an audience dressed up to the nines and thus able to draw attention away from the hall itself. A cacophony of unsuccessful applications of style. We made a careful study of all the additions and, in many cases, subtractions. A curious finding was that the hall is not dependent on luxurious materials. There's not a trace of marble in sight. The allure of the hall lies in its ornamental ceilings, pilasters and columns, as well as in the moulded surfaces of the walls. Covering those features with a coat of squidgy paint had done them no justice. In our opinion, reconstruction wasn't the way to go. We simply didn't have enough data. We opted for a new entity, one held together by a coherence of style.

Renovating while the show goes on was an aspect of our work for both the HEMA and De Bijenkorf, but the logistics were never so complex as they have been in this project. For five long months we worked mostly at night, with a team of forty or so balanced on the scaffolding and a blasphemous background of pop music blaring through the hall. Come seven-thirty in the morning, all signs of work were cleared away and the rehearsal could begin for that evening's concert. As the last notes of the performance faded into the night, the renovation team arrived, ready to resume their duties: technicians, plasterers, ornamental painters and gold-leaf specialists. During the day I stopped by to determine if the colours were exactly what we wanted; floodlights used for construction don't always reflect colour accurately.

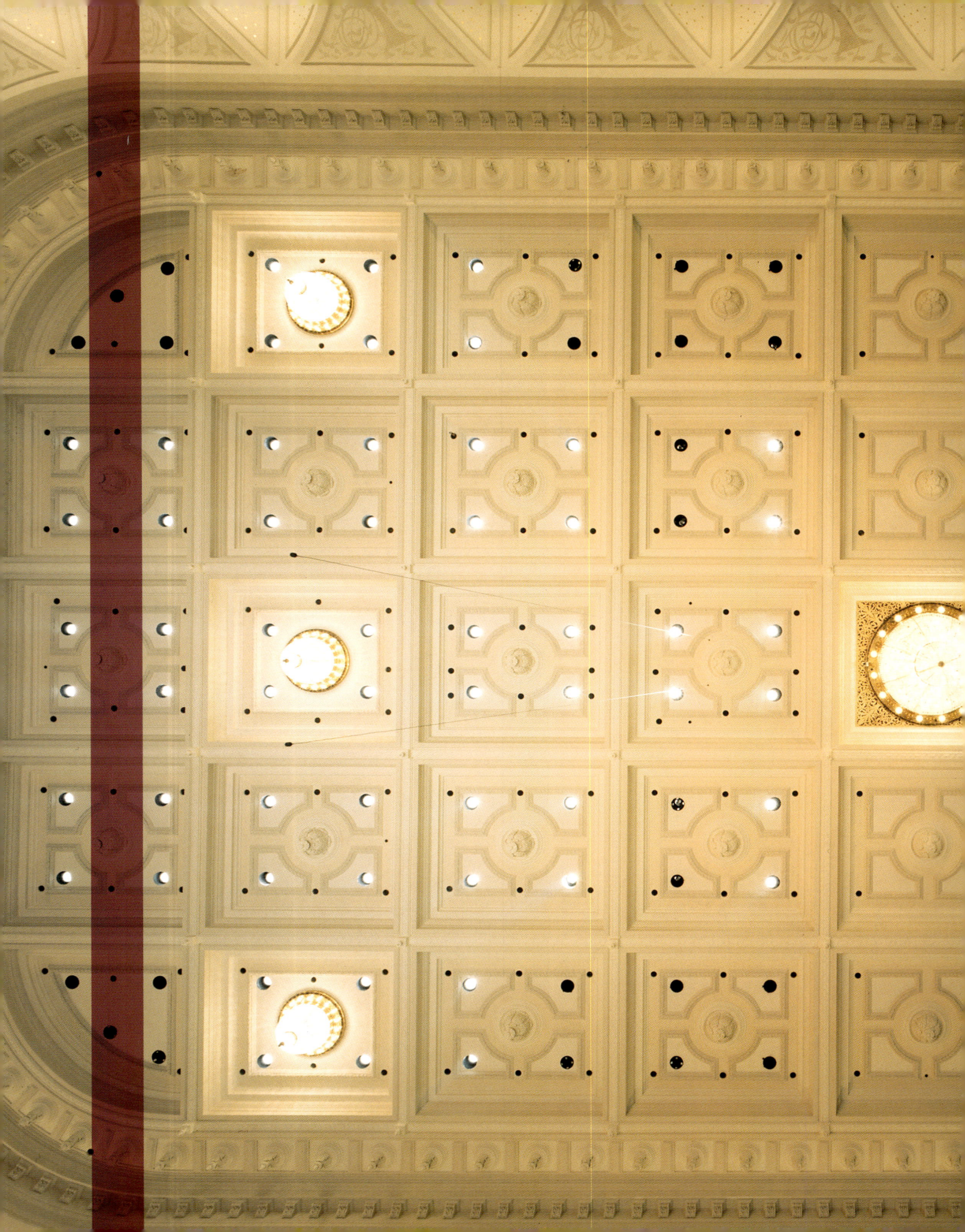

What have we done? The coffered ceiling is decorated once more, ornaments boast gold-leaf accents (we used 1200 booklets of gold leaf for a total of 192 square metres), the bearing function of cast-iron columns and pilasters is accentuated by a blue-green colour and, on the upper windows, arches dotted in gold twinkle like a starlit night. We developed a perforation programme that allows all sorts of technical installations (from hoisting and lighting systems to microphones) to be suspended from the ceiling. By using more than ten shades of white, cream and pale grey, we created a hall that sparkles.

Concealed behind this brief summary is an avalanche of decisions. Take the walls, which had to combine subtlety with opulence. If we opted for soft tints, we'd be knee-deep in pastels before we knew it. Definitely not what we wanted. If we selected brighter colours, the result would be overwhelming. In the end, we decided to use a palette of grey, beige and a blend of the two.

Okay. At that point we knew what we wanted, but that doesn't mean we had the right paint to do the job. Ultimately, a good starting point for a series of clear and muddy tints meant to complement one another turned out to be the bone-white colour of a cow's bone (straight from the slaughterhouse). The complexity of such decisions was why we deliberately rejected the idea of a structural engineer as head contractor, opting instead for Teun Bleijenberg of Restoration Atelier Rescura. We were duly impressed by a company that does plastering, gilding and glazing, but it was Teun's enormous enthusiasm that really convinced us.

Initially you simply don't realise that this hall is tremendously significant to a wide diversity of groups. Sharp-eyed observers watched every move we made. Attempting to tread on as few toes as possible, we presented our plans to a number of interested parties, including conductors Riccardo Chailly and Bernard Haitink, who were far more concerned about maintaining the renowned acoustics of the hall than about its appearance. For that reason, we brought in Dutch acoustics firm Peutz and later called on Arup Acoustics, for a second opinion.

A particularly thorny problem was the very limited opportunity we had to test our solutions on site. A considerable number of components were prepared with the help of computer simulations, but since results can never be predicted with absolute certainty, the whole project has been one tension-filled roller-coaster ride. The moment that the rear half of the hall, including the balcony, was finished, and we saw, at long last, that the subtle chromatic nuances had exactly the effect we wanted, was simultaneously exciting, solemn and glorious. Another moving moment was when we heard that the permanent members of the Royal Concertgebouw Orchestra, upon returning from summer recess, burst into spontaneous applause during their first rehearsal in the wholly transformed Main Hall.

The Main Hall is not the first section of the Concertgebouw that we tackled. And rightly so. Our first job was to gain the confidence of all parties involved. In 1996 we started with offices, restaurant and café facilities, and toilets; followed by the entire basement: greenroom, tuning rooms, and accommodations for conductors and soloists. The basement is a low space with many conduits, connections, cables and countless things that we couldn't move, such as the percussion studios, which are housed in a special soundproof concrete shell. We designed a new layout and, for most of the rooms, new furniture. Tuning rooms, for example, now have felt-lined compartments for the safe storage of instruments during intermissions.

We were aware, of course, that the Concertgebouw was a complicated commission, but the basement was a real baptism of fire. As we were to experience everywhere in this intensively used building, whatever we set out to do invariably disturbed something already in existence. A well-thought-out logistical plan was, therefore, of vital importance.

The gradual metamorphosis, which is to cover twelve years, is taking place both on stage and behind the scenes. Certain aspects are invisible. We spent a year, for instance, finding the ideal climate for the Main Hall. Or take the matter of doors. We counted eighty-eight types of doors at the outset; now all doors to the four stairwells have been identically repaired and provided with new technical components. It may not make the newspapers, but it's essential to the harmony of the building and to the fulfilment of current demands.

In 2006 the metamorphosis is to reach its culmination. But first we have to do the lobbies and corridors surrounding the Main Hall, the cloakroom, the choral hall, signage, soloist's rooms for the Recital Hall, the Recital Hall itself, et cetera, et cetera, et cetera.

Floors: MID Weaving Mill (custom-made carpet)
Ceiling and walls: Restoration Atelier Rescura and Teun Bleijenberg
Plasterers, A. Bok & Sons (manufacturer and supplier of paints),
KEIM Nederland (importer of mineral paints), Van Zoelen Painting,
Maintenance and Upholstery
Upholstery: Oostendorp Interior and Upholstery
Floor area: 12,400m²
Project duration: 10 years
Completion: 2006
Photography: Roos Aldershoff, Wim Dingemans/Silver Hands, Fas Keuzenkamp,
Pieter Vlamings

EPILOGUE

Since the days when architects considered interiors a minor aspect of the overall job – the general opinion when Evelyne Merkx set up her business in 1985 – many things have changed. The modernist tradition, which once had Calvinist Holland in its grip, was gradually forced to make way for a more consumer-orientated, commercial view of life. Enticement and entertainment have overtaken austerity and functionalism. The phenomenon has also affected architecture; a craving for comfort and amusement has paved the way for interior architecture.

Interior architects, as well as artists and designers, experiment with materials, with atmosphere, with tactility, decoration, ornament and even scent. An inherent aspect of the commercial race is the whirlpool of trends and hype to which it has given birth. By the time an interior appears in a magazine, it's practically obsolete. Though Merkx has plunged with complete dedication into the space now reserved for interior architecture, her approach to the interior is anything but trendy and fleeting. Working with an architect – of all people! – means she can combine her styling talent with his more spatial, architectonic interventions.

Mixed métiers make the team virtually unique in the Netherlands. A survey of the Low Countries uncovers only one other practice of this size with this particular sort of diversity – the Trude Hooykaas Design Group, an outfit strikingly similar to Merkx+Girod. A firm with the same hunger for new challenges, with the same willingness to experiment with new materials and techniques, and with the same love of craftsmanship. The designers at Trude Hooykaas show a preference for functionality. And their expertise covers both interior design and architectonic intervention. Another salient detail is that they, like Merkx+Girod, recently designed (in collaboration with Meyer and Van Schooten Architects) the headquarters of a major Dutch bank: ING. The ING House is less than a kilometre away from the main office of ABN AMRO, whose interior is a tribute to the talents of Merkx+Girod...

Clients see the advantages of this approach. As a consequence, these firms are breaking fresh ground in the profession. They are managing to acquire jobs that not long ago would have gone, without a second thought, to traditional architecture firms; when Evelyne Merkx entered the business, rarely was an interior architect an independent member of the group involved in a building project. Recognition of interior architecture as a specialism and of Merkx+Girod's methodology is also expressed in the invitation that Merkx+Girod received from the Eindhoven Design Academy. The Dutch school of design asked them to join the teaching staff of the master's programme offered by its Department of Interior Architecture.

Visitors to the Merkx+Girod website see projects, projects and more projects – a panoply of shops, restaurants and offices designed by this architecture firm. Don't look for philosophies, strategies or ground rules, however. The work must speak for itself. The same applies to real life. Basic principles and higher aims are part of the picture, of course. Merkx and Girod both believe, for instance, that interior architecture is a three-dimensional discipline. Colours, materials and elements designed for a certain project – purpose-built lamps or counters – are important, but they represent the finishing touches, not the heart of the design.

160

At the heart of the design is space, with light running a close second. No matter what kind of space the architects are confronted with – office, retail or domestic (the firm's residential projects are not included in this book) – they begin the design process by shaping and reshaping the floor plan until the space is as good as it gets, until daylight can penetrate the interior as deeply and abundantly as possible.

Another essential point of agreement between the two relates to their approach to historical buildings. Merkx+Girod Architects doesn't shy away from contemporary interventions. New is fine, as long as sound relationships and good proportions are maintained. Very early in their individual careers (long years of working alone or with others preceded their collaborative efforts), Merkx and Girod tackled various projects with a clever combination of renovation and innovation.

One of Merkx's first jobs – the renovation of the Grand Café Restaurant on Platform 2b, Amsterdam Central Station – was to adapt a 19th-century interior to meet the demands of a contemporary restaurant. She deliberately added modern elements to the existing interior. Patrice accomplished the same sort of feat early in his career. Together with Abel Cahen, his partner at the time, he designed the first modernist post-war building within Amsterdam's ring of canals. Their ideas were shockingly modern in the eyes of authorities responsible for the appearance of the city's buildings.

Characteristic of Merkx+Girod is an analytical approach to interior design. The architects begin by defining aesthetic, logistic and technical issues, after which they develop a master plan. The firm also thinks in terms of concepts and presentation strategies. One example is a Merkx+Girod initiative for HEMA, which linked the existing advertising material dropped in people's mailboxes with illustrated panels in the store. Another is the concept for Anna van Toor, a chain of fashion outlets for which the firm created an integral design that covered everything from interior to packaging. Certain suggestions related directly to the fashions themselves.

Reviews of the firm's work often refer to that 'characteristic Merkx+Girod style'. The reference is to the use of clear and vibrant colours, a preference for artisanal detail and the use of decorative graphic elements, such as Dutch words, set in tile, for the 'sausage' and 'cream slice' served in HEMA restaurants. By now, Evelyne and Patrice have grown used to having their work recognised in these finishing touches rather than in the spatial interventions they find so important.

Of course, styling is much easier to identify.

'HOW DO I FINISH IT OFF...?'

Yes, that's something I ask myself with great regularity. Take the Trêves Hall, for instance. The table alone is a building in itself. Extraordinarily complicated, because it has to be easy to dismantle. But once something's been designed and I see that it's good, I'm terribly happy.

EVELYNE MERKX

Sometimes I worry in the sense of: Is it going well? Are we on the right track? It's the same every time. When a project is done, you soon forget the moments that found you groping in the dark.

PATRICE GIROD

INSPIRATION

Want to talk about inspiration? Just imagine a project like *The Glory of the Golden Age*. God, was I happy to get that job. A commission like that prompts you to let everything go and learn to look at the world in a new way.

EVELYNE MERKX

STYLE

If you insist on pinning a style on our work, just call it 'simple chic'. Good materials applied attractively and logically.

EVELYNE MERKX

INDISCRIMINATE APPLICATION

You can't apply contemporary design indiscriminately to a building like the Concert-gebouw, which is actually not such a strong design. Adolf Leonard van Gendt used a mishmash of classical styles and apparently ran out of money before getting to the interior, with its display of standard items straight from catalogues issued by iron foundries and ornament manufacturers. After the opening in 1888, the hall waited ten years for a coat of paint (to brighten the coronation of Queen Wilhelmina).

EVELYNE MERKX

162

UGLY

EVELYNE MERKX

Occasionally I'm surprised when people link our name to the Concertgebouw. The project isn't even finished. We have five years to go. So, yes. Certain parts are still downright ugly.

CHAMPAGNE

PATRICE GIROD

Placing the champagne bar at the site of the original entrance – today's entrance is part of the new wing designed by Pi de Bruijn – was a good move.

SPECIFIC PROBLEMS + SPECIFIC SOLUTIONS

EVELYNE MERKX

Most of our work has to do with existing buildings, whose specific problems demand specific solutions. What should we do with these low ceilings? How can we deal with those unsightly windows? Such questions, combined with what the client wants from the space – that's the challenge.

HARD-BURNT TILE

EVELYNE MERKX

Hard-burnt baked tile? An outstanding tile, nothing more, nothing less. Good colours, nice hard material. Needs fine pointing. Absolutely. Berlage was a master in the use of these tiles. But I have no particular interest in them. They are in the Cookery Shop, however, as well cs in my own home. And the renovation that I'm working on at the moment – oh hell, they're part of that too!

QUESTIONS

EVELYNE MERKX

Routing takes top priority in a department store. The rest is display systems, display systems, display systems. From ring to rug, we have to make sure that every product is well displayed. How do customers want to view rugs? How can you prevent theft? Where do you store the stock on hand? These are the kinds of questions I ask myself.

DEPARTMENT STORE KNOW-HOW

EVELYNE MERKX

Light, too, is a vital factor in a department store. You need to create an abundance of light without calling attention to the fact. We often collaborate with a manufacturer (Erco, Philips) in designing the general lighting system. Anyone who's familiar with department-store design knows, for example, that the light in a fitting room should never be directly overhead. Light beaming straight down on customers make them look plump; it doesn't stimulate sales. And never forget – sales are what it's all about. Every square metre has to turn a profit. That doesn't leave much room for drama or special effects.

DOMESTIC

The special letterboxes and concrete lighting ornaments are features that we referred to as 'domestic detailing'. But I think that the long waiting time – we submitted our plan no less than ten times – had something to do with it as well.

PATRICE GIROD

PERSEVERANCE

The two in-house restaurants and the 'sandwich club' (quick-lunch counter) are like everything else in this project – it's okay, it's adequate, but it doesn't tug at my heart-strings. The only thing I really appreciate about the job is our perseverance.

EVELYNE MERKX

THE PERFECT COLOUR

We mixed up three different combinations of paint before finding the right shade of green. That's what it took to create the ideal dramatic setting for Rembrandt's famed civic guards.

EVELYNE MERKX

TAKING A LOOK

De Bijenkorf is a good client. The organisation is genuinely interested in realising something special. They've even sent us abroad. We went to London, for instance, to take a look at Harvey Nichols, where we feasted our eyes on the visual merchandising in that department store. But what's really nice is that nowadays foreign stylists and designers are showing up to take a look at De Bijenkorf.

EVELYNE MERKX

164

BIBLIOGRAPHY IN CHRONOLOGICAL ORDER

BOOKS

Architectuur in Nederland: Jaarboek 1989-1990. Netherlands Architecture Institute, Van Loghum Slaterus Publishers, the Netherlands, 1990.

Het oude westen Rotterdam: Laboratorium van de stadsvernieuwing. 010 Publishers, the Netherlands, 1993.

Van der Hoeven, Ernst. *De renovatie van de Grote Zaal van het Concertgebouw in Amsterdam.* Merkx+Girod B.V. and Rescura BV/T, Bleijenberg Stucadoor b.v., the Netherlands, 1999.

Din, Rasshied. *New Retail.* Conran Octopus Limited, UK, 2000.

MAGAZINES AND NEWSPAPERS

'Boekhandel te Amsterdam'. *bouwkundig weekblad*, 25 June 1968, 185-187.

'Woonhuis met garage te Amsterdam-Osdorp'. *bouwkundig weekblad*, 8 July 1969, 288-289.

van Heuvel, Wim J. 'Eigentijdse architectuur aan Amsterdamse singel'. *Cobouw*, 16 April 1971.

'Woningen te Amsterdam'. *Bouw*, 22 July 1978, 35-36.

'Bejaardencentrum te Amsterdam'. *Bouw*, 22 August 1981, 69-70.

'Woningen en winkels te Wassenaar'. *Bouw*, 30 October 1982, 48-50.

'Multifunctionele stadsvernieuwing te Rotterdam'. *Bouw*, 27 April 1985, 77-80.

'Woningbouw te Amersfoort'. *Bouw*, 12 April 1986, 35-38.

Wuestman, Gerdien. 'Niet als huis gebouwd, wel als huis bewoond'. *VT Wonen*, January 1988, 97-103.

Koster, Egbert. 'Woningbouwproject "Amsterdamse Poort" te Haarlem'. *de Architect*, April 1988, 53-57.

Elias, Mirjam. ' Ik wou en ik zou'. *de Volkskrant*, 12 November 1988.

'Roze toren bij Haarlemmerplein: woongebouw met uitstraling'. *de Architect*, February 1989, 69-73.

Slawik, Han. 'Im Jordaan'. *Deutsche Bauzeitung*, August 1991, 34-36.

Mens, Robert. 'Metamorfose van een huis'. *Marie Claire Wonen*, November 1991, 6-11.

De Haas, Annemarie. 'Kamers met karakter'. *VB Magazine*, April 1994, 44.

Osté, Mariëlle. 'Meesteres van de synthese'. *Elle Wonen*, April/May 1994, 42-48.

Papo, Jan Willem. 'Licht geeft flatteuze witheid'. *Eigen Huis & Interieur*, July 1994, 68-75.

'Als het goed is, hoor je meestal niets'. *PI, Projekt & Interieur*, April 1996, 84-87.

'Rotterdam eerste met nieuwe helderheid'. *PI, Projekt & Interieur*, February 1997, 32-35.

Melis, Liesbeth. 'Echt HEMA'. *de Architect*, March 1997, 88-89.

Feiter, Astrid. 'Interieurarchitecte Evelyne Merkx en de no nonsense van de HEMA'. *Opzij*, June 1997, 86-89.

De Vries, Marina. 'HEMA krijgt die frisse foldersfeer'. *Het Parool*, 18 June 1997, 19.

Van Zalingen, Marieke. 'Een oer-Hollandse winkel'. *Eigen Huis & Interieur*, December 1997, 78-80.

'Grote zaal krijgt ornamenten terug'. *de Volkskrant*, 30 January 1998.

'Akoestici waken over opknapbeurt'. *de Volkskrant*, 8 April 1998.

Telgenhof, Gerda. 'Concertgebouw krijgt ornamenten terug'. *NRC Handelsblad*, 8 April 1998.

'Grote Zaal straks zo goed als nieuw'. *Het Parool*, 8 April 1998.

Nauta, Hans. 'Vermoeide concertzaal gaat weer twinkelen'. *Trouw*, 15 July 1998.

Jansen, Kasper. 'Overal glanst nieuw bladgoud'. *NRC Handelsblad*, 14 August 1998.

Nagan, Doron. 'Concertgebouw straalt weer'. *Het Algemeen Dagblad*, 26 August 1998.

Huisman, Jaap. 'Grote Zaal is bevrijd van een grauwsluier'. *de Volkskrant*, 1 September 1998.

Kouters, Steffie. 'Eeuwige twijfelaar en lastpak'. *de Volkskrant*, 12 September 1998.

Jongenelen, S. 'Concertgebouw sprankelt als nooit tevoren'. *Het Financieele Dagblad*, 25 September 1998.

Bast, Truska. 'Belegen wit, dus geen kalkwit'. *Het Parool*, 29 September 1998.

'Discussie over spanningsveld tussen vorm en gebruik'. *Pl, Projekt & Interieur*, December 1998, 12-14.

Marshall, Jules. 'Building a Better Beehive'. *Frame*, March/April 1999, 35-45.

Ippel, Marjan. 'Mijn werk gaat niet alléén over winkels'. *Elle Wonen*, December 1998/January 1999, 50-52.

Grafe, Christoph. 'Interieurs van Merkx+Girod'. *de Architect*, April 1999, 95-99.

Van Osch, Brenda. 'Rust en een persoonlijk stempel'. *Elsevier*, May 1999, 74-82.

Brady, Rupert Parker. 'Ik hou van doe maar gewoon'. *Retailtribune*, 13 May 1999, 12-15.

De Graaf, Kees. ' Luxe wonen in Nederland'. *Bouw,* September 1999, 30-32.

Berkhout, Juliette. 'De smaakmaker/ Ik kijk altijd goed. Niet om het na te doen, maar om het anders te doen'. *VT Wonen*, October 1999, 10-11.

'Licht en leesplankjes voor Van Gogh museum'. *Pl, Projekt & Interieur*, October 1999, 76-81.

'ABN Amro en de kunst van het bankieren'. *Pl, Projekt & Interieur*, November/December 1999, 86-90.

Roes, Els. 'Ik breng orde in de chaos'. *De Telegraaf*, 5 November 1999, 19.

Ippel, Marjan. 'Kleurbehandeling'. *Elle Wonen*. April 2000, 134-138.

'Portret'. *Living*, February/March 2000, 131.

Lamoree, Jhim and Marina de Vries. 'De Gouden Eeuw gaat nooit verloren'. *Het Parool*, 11 March 2000.

Thiemann, Robert. 'Vibrant Workbook'. *Frame*, March/April 2000, 106.

Slijkerman, Diederick. 'Merkx+Girod: architecten voor de Raad van State'. *Ter State*, 28 April 2000, 6-10.

Van Gessel, Marieke. ' Interieurarchitect Evelyne Merkx'. *Residence*, July/August 2000, 36-37.

Van Zalingen, Marieke. 'Gracia Lebbink & Evelyne Merkx'. *Eigen Huis & Interieur*, July 2000, 21-23.

Van Zalingen, Marieke. 'Evelyne Merkx & Claudy Jongstra'. *Eigen Huis & Interieur*, August 2000, 45-47.

'Verzachting in de interieurarchitectuur'. *Pl, Projekt & Interieur*, December 2000, 112-113.

Sibarani, Marieke. 'Streepje voor'. *Elle Wonen*, October 2001, 67-70.

Rodermond, Janny. 'Eigen traditie van Merkx+Girod'. *de Architect*, May 2000, 18-25.

Douqué, Anne. 'ArboNed, waar mensen werken' (booklet accompanying the opening of ArboNed in Utrecht), 21 September 2001.

Koster, Egbert. 'Opmerkelijk maatwerk'. *Het Financieele Dagblad*, 6 October 2001.

Brummelman, Niels. 'Interview Evelyne Merkx: "Ik kan een echte lastpak zijn"'. *Business in Office*, December 2001, 16-20.

Posthuma, Sjoukje. 'Op zoek naar harmonie. De herinrichting van de Trêveszaal', *Smaak*, April 2002, 39-42.

Rodermond, Janny. 'Interieur Trêveszaal door Merkx+Girod', *de Architect*, May 2002, 87-91.

'Retail en branding: de nieuwe verzuiling, *Stedebouw & Architectuur*, July 2002, 4-5.

Grevers, Arie.'Waardige ruimtes' Interview Merkx en Verschuren, *Projekt+*, September 2002, 6-12.

169

PETER BIL'AK (1973) studied in Slovakia, the UK, the USA, France and the Netherlands. He now runs his own design studio in The Hague, an outfit equally at home in the worlds of culture and commerce. Projects range from editorial and graphic design to the creation of typefaces and websites. Bilak designed several fonts for FontShop. His Fedra Mono font, used in this book, is one of a number of typefaces distributed by his independent foundry, Typotheque.com. A co-founder and editor of *DOT DOT DOT* magazine, Bil'ak has lectured internationally; he currently teaches part-time at the Royal Academy in The Hague (Type & Media, a postgraduate course) and at the Arnhem Art Academy.

BRIGITTE VAN MECHELEN (1964) has university degrees in both art history and cultural studies. She also studied at the Utrecht Art Academy for three years. Her professional experience includes a position as editor at a small publishing company, where she specialised in the fields of interior architecture and contract furnishing. Van Mechelen currently works as a freelance journalist. Her articles on design and the visual arts appear regularly in publications such as *Items*, *Museumvisie*, *Man* and *Living*.

173

174

MERKX+GIROD: INTERIOR ARCHITECTS
Frame Monographs of Contemporary Interior
Architects

PUBLISHERS
Frame Publishers
www.framemag.com
Birkhäuser – Publishers for Architecture
www.birkhauser.ch

GRAPHIC DESIGN
Peter Biľak
www.peterb.sk

WRITTEN BY
Brigitte van Mechelen

COPY EDITING
Donna de Vries-Hermansader

TRANSLATION
InOtherWords: Donna de Vries-Hermansader

PRODUCTION
Tessa Blokland, *Frame* magazine,
Sylvia van Duyvenboode, Merkx+Girod Architects

COLOUR REPRODUCTION
Graphic Link

PRINTING
Veenman drukkers

WITH SPECIAL THANKS TO
Het Concertgebouw, Amsterdam; ArboNed, Utrecht;
HEMA, Amsterdam; De Bijenkorf, Amsterdam
Southeast Amstelveen; Van Gogh Museum Shop,
Amsterdam; ABN AMRO, Amsterdam; Anna van
Toor, Meerkerk; Trimp & van Tartwijk Property
Performance, IJsselstein; and Railinfrabeheer,
Verkeersleiding and Railned, Utrecht.

DISTRIBUTION
Benelux, China, Japan, Korea and Taiwan
ISBN 90-806445-9-5
Frame Publishers
Lijnbaansgracht 87hs
NL-1015 GZ Amsterdam
The Netherlands
www.framemag.com

All other countries
ISBN 3-7643-6744-X
Birkhäuser – Publishers for Architecture
P.O. Box 133
CH-4010 Basel
Switzerland
Member of the BertelsmannSpringer Publishing
Group
www.birkhauser.ch

Printed on acid-free paper produced from
chlorine-free pulp. TCF ∞
Printed in the Netherlands.
987654321